The Seventy Sevens Prophecy Told to Daniel by The Angel Gabriel

By
Douglas W. Ophus

FUTURE HISTORY BEFORE IT HAPPENS BOOKS

The Seventy Sevens Prophecy Told to Daniel by The Angel
Gabriel

Unless otherwise noted scriptures are from the New King James Version
(Nashville: Thomas Nelson Inc., 1982)

Other scriptures quoted
The Interlinear NIV Hebrew-English Old Testament, John R. Kohlenberger III,
(Grand Rapids: Zondervan Publishing House, 1987)

The Interlinear Bible, Hebrew-Greek-English, Jay P. Green Sr., general editor
and translator, (Hendrickson Publishers, 1986)

The Interlinear Greek-English New Testament, The Reverend Alferd Marshall
(London: Samuel Bagster and Sons Lim., 1958)

The Septuagint with Apocrypha, Greek, and English, (Grand Rapids:
Zondervan Publishing House, 1978)

Other references are footnoted or end noted.

Published by
FUTURE HISTORY BEFORE IT HAPPENS BOOKS LLC

www.futurehistorybeforeithappensbooks.com

Library of Congress Cataloging-in-Publication Data
Ophus, Douglas W.
The Seventy Sevens Prophecy Told to Daniel by The Angel
Gabriel

ISBN-13: 978-0-578-42819-2

Printed in the United States of America

Introduction

The Seventy Sevens prophecy begins in Daniel 9:24 and continues through Daniel 9:27. Daniel 9:24 is a preface to the counting of the seventy sevens that speaks of several wonderful aspects of the accomplishments of the Messiah for the people. It is an insight into how to interpret the work of the Messiah who was cut off, but not for Himself. The preface has been wrongly interpreted by modernist interpreters by saying that there are three negative phrases and three positive phrases and then applying the negative phrases to the people. On the contrary they are all positive phrases that are aspects of the accomplishments of the Messiah for the people. For example, the phrase saying, **"to make atonement for wickedness, iniquity,"** is a wonderful aspect of the work of the Messiah for the people. The seventy sevens prophecy is amazingly accurate, too. It not only tells that the Messiah will be cut off; it also tells when He will be cut off by means of the counting of the seven sevens and sixty-two sevens, and why He will be cut off in the preface to the counting of the seventy sevens.

The seventy sevens prophecies are interrelated in their order of succession with the fulfillment of each one following from the fulfillment of the previous one. **The Messiah, the Ruler, comes**. As the anointed one, he has a mission, and it is that **the Messiah will be cut off, but not for himself.** He was cut off out of the land of the living **to make atonement for wickedness, iniquity.** He fulfilled the sacrifices of the temple once for all **to bring in everlasting righteousness.** Those who believe in the Messiah [Christ] are born again with the indwelling of the Holy Spirit and are the Temple of God. Since God has moved his residence from the temple building to indwell his people, the enemy took opportunity and **the people of the prince to come will destroy the city and the sanctuary.** In the seventy sevens prophecy there are more that follow that are in this book.

During the Exodus of 'the children of Israel' from Egypt as is described in the Torah [the law] in Leviticus 25:2, the Lord spoke to Moses on Mount Sinai saying, **"Speak to the children of Israel, and say to them: 'When you come into the land which I will give to you, then the land shall keep a Sabbath to the Lord.'"**

On each seventh year they were to observe a sabbath rest of the land; they were to neither plant nor prune their vineyard. After, the children of Israel entered the land given to them by the Lord, they neglected to observe 'the sabbath rest of the land to the Lord' for many years, even until the time of Jeremiah the prophet. Jeremiah prophesied that the land shall be a desolation for seventy years. The people taken captive to Babylon would facilitate the observance of the seventy sabbath rests of the land that had not been observed by the children of Israel.

Jeremiah 25:11

11 And this whole land shall be a desolation *and* an astonishment, and these nations shall serve the king of Babylon seventy years.

Daniel and Ezekiel were among the captives in Babylon. The army of Nebuchadnezzar, king of Babylon, destroyed the city of Jerusalem and tore down its walls. The land was left desolate. While being a captive in Babylon, Daniel had been reading Jeremiah as he said in Daniel 9:2 … **I, Daniel, understood by the books the number of the years *specified* by the word of the Lord through Jeremiah the prophet, that He would accomplish seventy years in the desolations of Jerusalem.**

Daniel understood by reading the prophet Jeremiah that He (the Lord) would accomplish seventy years of desolations of Jerusalem. Daniel prayed to the Lord God for more understanding.

Daniel 9:3

3 Then I set my face toward the Lord God to make request by prayer and supplications, with fasting, sackcloth, and ashes.

While Daniel was in prayer, the angel Gabriel appeared to him and told him the seventy weeks [seventy sevens] prophecy.

Daniel 9:25

25 "Know therefore and understand, *that* from the going forth of the command to restore and build Jerusalem until Messiah the Prince, *there shall be* seven weeks and sixty-two weeks; The street shall be built again, and the wall, even in troublesome times.

The counting of the seven weeks [seven sevens] and sixty-two weeks [sixty-two sevens] until the Messiah the Prince [Ruler] appears, begins from the going forth of the command to restore and build Jerusalem with streets and a wall. The sevens are interpreted as a 'group of seven years' (not days), since the prophecy made by Jeremiah was for seventy years and the prophecy made by Gabriel to Daniel is seven times longer.

Nehemiah was a descendant of those taken captive from Judah to Babylon. He was the cupbearer of King Artaxerxes and he was sad because the walls of Jerusalem were still broken down. Artaxerxes seeing Nehemiah's sadness, gave Nehemiah letters that give him authority to go to Judah and allowed him the use of materials to build the wall around Jerusalem. The most plausible event that marks the beginning of the counting of the seventy sevens prophecy is the letters given by Artaxerxes I to Nehemiah. Nehemiah states that he received the letters from Artaxerxes in the month of Nisan in the 20th year of Artaxerxes. Hebrews from Judah used the seventh month for beginning the counting of the year of the king, but the Babylonians used the first month for the beginning of the counting of the year of the king. Therefore, the 20th year of Artaxerxes according to Nehemiah, who was a descendant from Judah, was the 21st year according to the Babylonians.

This book is the first book[1:1] (that I am aware of) that correctly uses the Julian date for the 21st year of Artaxerxes I in the month of Nisan as April 3-May 1, 444 B.C. Julian according to *Babylonian Chronology 626 B.C.-A.D. 75* by Richard A. Parker and Waldo H. Dubberstein, page 32.[1:2]

The book of Revelation gives us insight into Daniels prophetic use of the 360-day year. This book calculates in Chapters 8 and 9, the seven sevens and sixty-two sevens of years beginning with Nisan 1 (April 3) 444 B.C. using both the Julian and the ancient Babylonian calendars, while in both cases adjusting for a 360-day year. The calculation arriving at March 30, 33 A.D., the exact date of the triumphal entry of Jesus through the Eastern Gate.

This book includes the whole seventy sevens prophecy given to Daniel by the angel Gabriel and includes much of the theological implications. It teaches the sufficiency of the Messiah, the Ruler, Jesus' sacrificial atoning death on the cross.

It explains, **"So will the son of man be three days and three nights in the heart of the earth"** spoken of by Jesus according to Matthew 12:40b, which has perplexed many.

It speaks of the dark as night for three hours from the sixth hour (noon) until the ninth hour (3 p.m.) while Jesus was on the cross and includes extrabiblical historical references to it and the earthquake spoken of in the gospels.

It mentions Joel's prophecy found in the Old Testament that was referred to by the disciple/apostle Peter in Acts 2:20, **"The sun shall be turned into darkness, and the moon into blood,"** of which a red moon eclipse the evening Jesus was crucified, April 3, 33 A.D. has been verified by astronomical calculations.

It includes a summary of the destruction of Jerusalem and the Temple according to the Jewish historian Flavius Josephus in his *The Jewish Wars*, who was an eye witness.

I:1. There was a groundbreaking book *Chronological Aspects of the Life of Christ* by Harold W. Hoehner, groundbreaking because it correctly converted the 20th year of Artaxerxes according to the way Nehemiah counted it to the 21st year according to the way the Babylonians counted it, as Nisan 444 B.C. Julian. However, it used March 5 as the beginning date and the calculation of the span of years concluded 25 days before March 30, 33 A.D., and then added 25 days (pp. 137-139).

I:2. Based on clay tablets with observations of the sun and the moon during the reign of a certain king found by archaeologists and the works of other interpreters, Richard A. Parker and Waldo H. Dubberstein wrote *Babylonian Chronology 626 B.C.-A.D. 75*. On page 32, the 21st year of Artaxerxes I in the month of Nisanu [Nisan, Hebrew] is 4/3-5/1 (April 3-May 1) 444 B.C. Julian.

Letters have been found at Elephantine, Egypt written in Aramaic by the Hebrews that lived there. Some are double dated with the Egyptian solar date and the Persian king date using the 7th month as the first year of the king in the same way as Nehemiah. Then based on those findings Siegfried H. Horn and Lynn H. Wood wrote *The Chronology of Ezra 7* and on page 158, the 20th year of Artaxerxes I in the month of Nisan is 4/2-5/1 (April 2-May 1) 444 B.C. Thus, the two methods confirm each other within one day of each other, see chapters 8 and 9 for more details.

The author Douglas Ophus, B.A., M.A. in Theological Studies.

Table of Contents

Chapter 1

The mostly counterclockwise solar system, the Jewish lunar calendar and the 360-day future year

The planet earth rotates on its axis counterclockwise and orbits the sun in a counterclockwise direction. The rotation of the earth causes it to function like a gyroscope; its axis maintains the same direction relative to the stars throughout the earth's orbit. As per National Weather Service diagrams: "the northern axis of the earth is tilted 23.5° toward the sun during the Summer Solstice in the northern hemisphere, June 20-22, and away from the sun 23.5° during the Winter Solstice in the northern hemisphere, December 21-22. During the Vernal Equinox, March 20-21, and the Autumnal Equinox, September 22-23, days and nights are the same length due to the north and south of the axis of the earth being equally inline with the orbit of the earth."[1]

"The angular diameter of the moon as measured from earth is .5°."[2] The sun and the moon have the same apparent angle of about .5° as is apparent during an eclipse of the sun. "We now know that the sun is almost 400 times further away than the moon."[2]

The orbit of the earth is slightly elliptical. "At perihelion, the closest point, the earth is 91.4 million miles from the sun on Jan. 3 and at aphelion, the furthest point, the earth is 94.5 million miles from the sun."[3] "Even though the earth is closer to the sun during summer in the southern hemisphere than it is during summer in the northern hemisphere, summers in the northern hemisphere are 4° F. warmer due to a greater land mass absorbing sunlight."[3]

One might expect that the gravitational attraction of the sun would pull the earth closer and closer to the sun, but it doesn't because "the sun is traveling counterclockwise 4,400 miles per hour at the equator"[4] and revolves on its axis "one revolution in 26.6 days."[4] The counterclockwise rotation of the sun adds torque to the counterclockwise orbit of earth that counterbalances the gravitational attraction of the sun and the earth is actually moving away from the sun, but at a nearly imperceptible amount.

A 360° revolution of the earth around the sun takes 365.24219 days, so the earth orbits 360° ÷ 365.24219 days = .9856° per day around the sun. As the earth rotates 360° counterclockwise on its axis, it needs to rotate an additional .9856° to be at the same point relative to the sun in a 24 hour day.

The moon revolves on its axis counterclockwise and orbits around the earth counterclockwise. "*At apogee*, the furthest point, the moon is 252,088 miles from earth and *at perigee*, the closest point, the moon is 225,623 miles from earth."[5]. "Both points *perigee and apogee* of the moon's orbit advance eastward around the earth completing a full cycle in about 412 days or almost 14 lunar months."[6]

"The lunar orbital plane *around the earth* is tilted about 5° 9' *north and south* relative to the ecliptic (mean value)."[6] The moon crosses the orbital plane of the earth twice each month, once as it ascends northward and again as it descends southward, where it crosses cycles with the perigee and apogee.

There is a bulge of the ocean on the side of the earth nearest to the moon. As the earth rotates the bulge adds torque to the moon and causes the moon to speed up slightly and as a result that the size of the orbit of the moon is increasing slightly each year.

The bulge causes the ocean tides and the friction of the tides on the surface of the earth causes the rotation of the earth to slow "such that mean solar days get longer by 1.75 milliseconds per century."[6]

One complete revolution of the moon with respect to the stars is called a Sidereal Month. "The lunar orbital period with respect to the stars (Sidereal Month) is 27.32166 days."[7].

During the period in which the moon has orbited around the earth in one revolution, the earth has orbited around the sun almost one thirteenth of a revolution, so the moon needs to travel slightly more than two days more around the earth in order to be at the same point relative to the sun.

The Synodic Month is the time it takes the moon to orbit the earth one revolution plus the time needed to be at the same point relative to the sun. "The mean length of the Synodic Month is 29.53059 days."[7] When the moon is in line between the earth and the sun, it is in conjunction with the sun. When the moon is in conjunction, the dark side of the moon is facing the earth and it is not visible in the sky.

When the moon is in conjunction and crossing the orbital plane of the earth at perigee, (the closest point to the earth), and the sun is at aphelion, (the farthest point from the earth), there is a total eclipse of the sun as viewed from earth.

The moon advances east 360° ÷ 27.32166 days = 13.1763° each day with respect to the stars, and the sun advances east .9856° each day with respect to the stars, so the moon advances 13.1763° - .9856° = 12.19° faster than the sun each day or 12.19° ÷ 24 hours per day = .5° per hour faster than the sun.

Since the apparent diameter of the moon as viewed from earth is an angle of .5°, then each hour the moon moves across the sky is one moon diameter faster than the sun. Based on that when the moon approaches the sun in the sky, it would take one hour to be in conjunction with the sun and another hour to be on the other side of the sun, but that is not visible in the sky except during an eclipse of the sun.

When the moon is in conjunction with the sun during the day-time it is not visible in the sky as viewed from the earth. The moon is not visible after sunset either because when the sun is over the horizon the moon has not advanced sufficiently away from the glare of the sun to be seen just after sunset.

The next day after the moon is in conjunction with the sun, the moon has separated sufficiently from the sun such that after sunset the sun can no longer be seen over the horizon, but when the weather is clear the moon reflecting the sun can be seen for a while until it also disappears over the horizon due to the spinning of the earth. Since the moon is spherical, the illuminated side of the moon appears to have a crescent shape as viewed from the earth.

Chapter 1: The mostly counterclockwise solar system, quotations
1. The Seasons, the Equinox, and the Solstices, www.weather.gov/cle/seasons
2. Understanding Astronomy: The Moon and Eclipses,
http://physics.weber.edu/schroeder/ua/MoonAndEclipses.html
3. Perihelion and aphelion, https://wikipedia.org/wiki/perihelion_and_aphelion
4. How fast does the sun spin? Spacemath@NASA
http://spacemath.gsfc.nasa.gov/weekly/4page1.pdf
5. How far away is the moon? NASA Space Place
https://spaceplace.nasa.gov/moon-distance/en/
6. The Length of the Lunar Cycle, Dr. Irv Bromberg, Univ. of Toronto, Canada,
http://www.sym454.org/lunar/
7. NASA-Eclipses and the Moon's Orbit, Fred Espenak, NASA's GSFC
https://eclipse.gsfc.gov/SEhelp/moonorbit.html

The moon in conjunction with the sun

When the
conjunction
sun while
the orbital
the earth and
is at its closest
the sun is at its
point a total
the sun occurs.
The diameter
is about 400
than the
the moon. The
400 times further
the moon.

moon is in
with the
crossing
plane of
the moon
point and
furthest
eclipse of

of the sun
times larger
diameter of
sun is about
away than

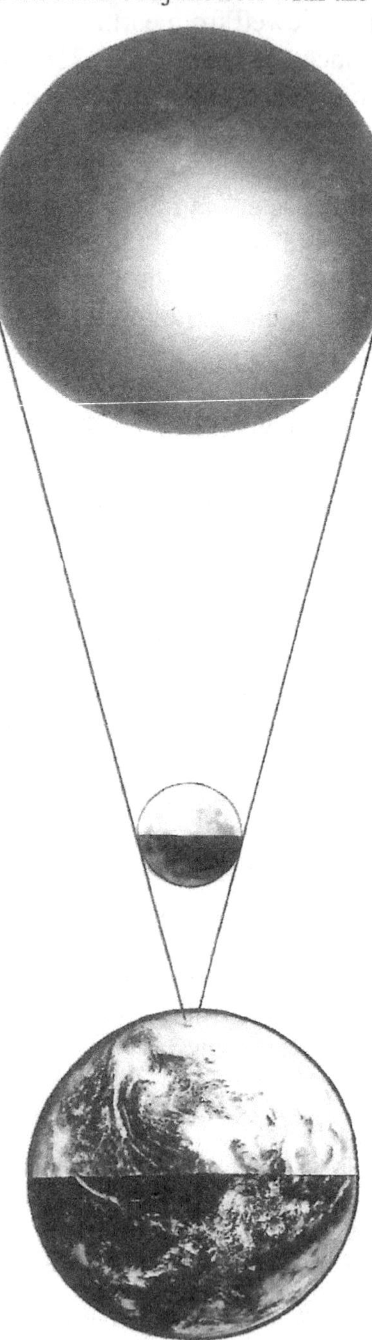

Not to scale

A new waxing crescent moon marks the beginning of a new
month on the   Jewish
lunar calendar

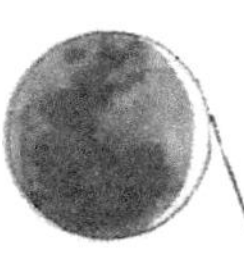

After the sun   disappears
over the horizon a   new
crescent moon is   visible for a
short time until it too   disappears
over the horizon due   to the
rotation of the earth
counterclockwise
Not to scale

The orbit of the moon around the earth is offset 5° 9' compared to the orbit plane of the earth around the sun.
The perigee (furthest point) and apogee (closest point) of the moon's slightly elliptical orbit cycles around the earth, completing a cycle in about 412 days. The moon crosses the orbit plane of the earth twice each month, once going below the orbit plane of the earth and again going above the orbit plane of the earth. If the moon happens to cross the orbit plane of the earth while the moon is in conjunction with the sun there is an eclipses of the sun.

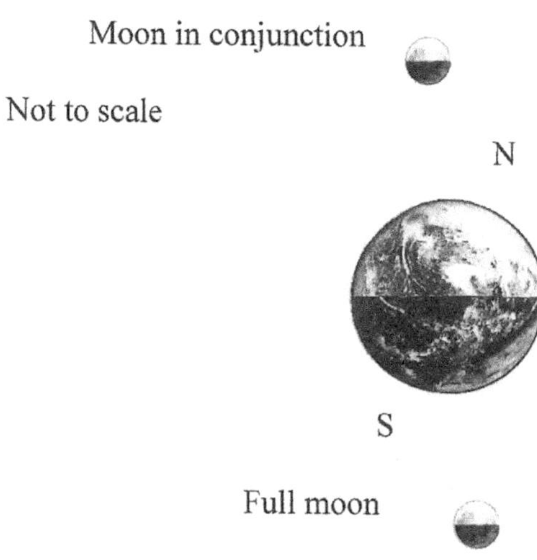

The Jewish Lunar Calendar

When the moon is in conjunction with the sun and not visible in the sky, modern writers refer to it as a new moon. They measure the length of a month from conjunction to conjunction.

Ancient people that used lunar calendars would not have thought of it that way. For ancient people that used lunar calendars, after the night the moon was not visible, on a following night the first crescent visible after sunset marked the beginning of a new month. As the sun disappeared over the horizon due to the rotation of the earth the illuminated side of the moon would appear as a crescent for a short time until it too disappeared over the horizon. This worked well for the Jews because they counted the beginning of a new day at sunset and it lasted until the next sunset. Sometimes they referred to it as a night and a day or a day and a night.

The average length of a lunar month is 29.530 days. In order to arrive at an average of 29½ days long the Jewish months alternate between 29 and 30 days long. The 12-month lunar year is 254 days long, 11 days shorter than the 365-day solar year. In order to compensate for seasonal drift a month was added every two or three years.

In the Bible in Genesis the months are referred to by a number, for example: Gen. 7:1 second month, Gen. 8:4 seventh month, Gen. 8:3 first month, and Gen. 8:4 second month.

When the Lord spoke to Moses and Aaron concerning the first Passover, He said that this month is to be counted as the first month. Exodus 12:2

2 This month *shall be* your beginning of months; it *shall be* the first month of the year to you.

On the tenth day of this month, they shall choose a male Lamb without blemish. On the fourteenth day they shall kill it at twilight then roast it in fire and eat it that night, which counts as the next day, the Lord's Passover, since the Jewish day begins at sunset.

Then after the first Passover, the Israelites exited Egypt led by Moses and traveled in the wilderness for forty years. While they were on their journey, the people celebrated the Passover, and Moses called the month, **Abib**, according to Exodus 13:4. While they were in the wilderness, God commanded them to build a tabernacle in a certain way and they performed offerings in it.

Numbers 29:1-6 describes the Feast of Trumpets on the first day of the seventh month as a day of blowing trumpets. Num. 7:11 describes the offerings on the Day of Atonement on the tenth day of the seventh month, and Num. 7:12 speaks of the offerings of the Feast of Tabernacles on the fifteenth day of the seventh month.

Before the Israelites entered the land promised to them, they were commanded by God to observe a sabbath rest of the land. Every seven years they were to rest the land and not plant.

The calendar during the days of Solomon

During the time of Solomon, the month of the Passover in the spring continued to be counted as the first month in the counting of the months that began the ecclesiastical year; however, the seventh month in the fall was the beginning of a new year that was used in civil matters for counting the year of the king. In order to keep the religious holy days the same distance apart, an intercalary month could not be placed between the first month and the seventh month.

The pre-exile calendar after Solomon

After the death of Solomon, in (932/931 B.C.[8]) the Northern Kingdom of Israel broke away from the Southern Kingdom of Judah, where Jerusalem was located, over the issue of taxes.

Under the leadership of Jeroboam I who had come from Egypt, the northern kingdom broke away from Judah. Jeroboam I set up idols for the people of the Northern Kingdom to worship, so they would not need to travel to Jerusalem. The Northern Kingdom began counting the first month as the New Year.

Judah continued to use the seventh month for counting the year of the king. The book of 2 Kings uses the seventh month for counting the year of the king.

The people of the Northern Kingdom were taken captive by the Assyrians and carried away. The Northern Kingdom ended in (723/722 B.C.[9]) before Judah was taken captive to Babylon.

From the time the Israelites entered the land until the time of the prophet Jeremiah, who was in Judah, the Israelites had not kept the sabbath rest of the land. Jeremiah prophesied that the land would become a desolation and the people would serve the king of Babylon for seventy years.

The calendar during the Babylonian exile

In fulfillment of the words out of the mouth of the prophet Jeremiah, the people were taken captive to Babylon so the land could have its seventy years of Sabbath rest.

Nebuchadnezzar, king of Babylon, made Jehoiakim, king of Judah, his vassal in 605 B.C.[10] Jehoiakim remained king; however, Daniel was among the earliest group taken captive.

After Jehoiakim was killed, his son Jehoiachin became king. Nebuchadnezzar came against Judah and Jehoiachin surrendered; he was taken captive and exiled to Babylon along with the prophet Ezekiel on Nisan 10 in the eighth year of Nebuchadnezzar (April 22, 597 B.C.[11]). During the Babylonian captivity, the prophet Ezekiel used the anniversary of the exile of Jehoiachin for dating the years.

In chapter 2, the Babylonian captivity is described in more detail.

During the captivity in Babylon the people of Judah adopted the Babylonian names for the months. The Babylonians counted the month of Nisanu, which was in the spring, as the first month and the beginning of the New Year for counting the year of the king.

Babylonian   Jewish
Full year   Full year
Nisanu   30 days   Nisan (1st month begins new year for Babylonians and begins ecclesiastical year for people from Judah)
Aiaru   29 days   Iyyar
Simanu   30 days   Sivan
Duzu   29 days   Tammuz
Abu   30 days   Ab
Ululu   29 days   Elul
Ululu II*   30 days   *(intercalary month), (sometimes)
Tashritu   30 days   Tishri (7th month begins civil year for counting year of the king for people from Judah)
Arahsamnu   29 or 30 day Heshvan
Kislimu   30 or 29 day Kislev
Tebetu   29 days   Tebeth
Shabatu   30 days   Shebat
Addaru   29 days   Adar I*   30 days
Addaru II*   30 days   Adar II   29 days (replaces Adar)

In a full year [leap year] the month of Adar I is added and the original Adar becomes Adar II. Religious holy days that are celebrated in the month of Adar are celebrated in Adar II.

The people from Judah counted the year of Nebuchadnezzar six months earlier than the Babylonians.

Nebuchadnezzar ascended to the throne just before the 7th month, the month of Tishri, so the people from Judah counted each year of king Nebuchadnezzar beginning with the month of Tishri, six months earlier than the year of the king according to the Babylonians, who began counting with the month of Nisanu.

The post exilic calendar used by those returning to Judah after the Babylonian captivity

The post exilic period refers to the time after Babylon was conquered by the Persian king Cyrus the Great. In the first year of his reign over Babylon, Cyrus made a proclamation releasing many captives to return to Judah (538/557 B.C.[12]), according to Isaiah's prophecy, to build on the city and lay the foundation of the Temple.

The captives released by Cyrus to return to Judah used the year of the Persian king as the year of the king with the month of Tishri as the New Year. That is supported by the Elephantine Letters with double dating according to the year of the Persian king and the Egyptian solar calendar found by archaeologists at Elephantine Egypt.

The post exiles in Judah had many difficulties with squatters that had moved in and the land was not producing good crops. The people had not been building on the temple and God sent Haggai to tell them to begin building on the temple. When the foundation of the temple was laid it coincided with the end of the seventy years of desolation of the land and Haggai pronounced a blessing on them that the land would grow good crops again.

The prophet Haggai used the Persian king Darius I for dating the year of the king based on the first month as the new year.

Quite the opposite to the case of Nebuchadnezzar, the counting of the year of Artaxerxes I is six months earlier by the Persians than by the people from Judah.

Artaxerxes I ascended to the throne after the month of Tishri, but before the month of Nisanu. The Persians begin counting the first year of Artaxerxes I with the month of Nisanu, six months before the people from Judah, who began counting the first year of Artaxerxes I with the month of Tishri

During the reign of Artaxerxes I, Ezra and Nehemiah were in Persia. Ezra went to Judah before Nehemiah. Ezra was concerned with an early establishment of the canon of the Hebrew scriptures.

Artaxerxes I gave Nehemiah letters for materials and authority to build the wall around the city of Jerusalem. Nehemiah's use of Tishri as the new year for counting the year of the king is one of the most sure cases in the Bible because the order of the months Nehemiah speaks of in the same year of the king is only possible when Tishri is the new year.

That is important to know because that is pertinent to the study of the fulfillment of the seventy sevens prophecy told to Daniel by the angel Gabriel.

During the first century A.D. the Sadducees were in charge of declaring the beginning of a new Jewish month. After at least two witnesses saw a new crescent moon, a new month was declared. In deciding a full year [leap year], the barley harvest and many other factors were taken into consideration.

Eventually the 19-year cycle was developed where years 3, 6, 8, 11, 14, 17 and 19 were made full years [leap years] then every 19 years the Jewish calendar agreed with the solar calendar.

Chapter 1: The Jewish lunar calendar, quotations
8. Jack Finegan, *Handbook of Biblical Chronology* (Hendrickson Publishers Inc., Peabody MA., 1999) p. 249 § 429   932/931 B.C. (Death of Solomon).
9. Ibid., p. 250 § 426
  723/722 B.C. (Northern Kingdom ended).
10. Ibid., p. 254 § 43   605 B.C. (Jehoiakim made vassal of Nebuchadnezzar; Daniel taken captive to Babylon, as per Daniel 1:1 in the third year of Jehoiakim).
11. Ibid., p. 257 § 440 and p. 262 § 447   April 22, 597 B.C. (Jehoiachin and Ezekiel exiled to Babylon).
12. Ibid., p. 266 § 454   538/557 B.C. (In the first year of his reign [over Babylon] Cyrus released many captives to return to Judah to build on Jerusalem and the temple, as per Ezra 1:1-11)

The 360-day future year

Much of the background to the New Testament book of Revelation is the Old Testament book of Daniel.

Revelation 11:2 and 13:5 speak of 42 months. Revelation 12:14 speaks of a time, times, and half-a-time. Revelation 11:3 and 12:6 speak of one thousand two hundred sixty days. A time, times, and half-a-time is interpreted to add up to $1 + 2 + \frac{1}{2} = 3\frac{1}{2}$ years; 42 months divided by 12 months per year equals $3\frac{1}{2}$ years, the same as a time, times, and half-a-time.

Revelation 12:6 and 12:14 refer to the same event, but the time span involved is measured in different ways. Revelation 12:6 speaks of the woman being fed in the wilderness 1260 days. Revelation 12:14 speaks of the woman that fled into the wilderness being nourished a time, times, and half-a-time or $3\frac{1}{2}$ years. Thus, 1260 days divided by $3\frac{1}{2}$ years equals 360 days per year. 360 days per year divided by 12 months per year equals 30 days per month. Therefore, the book of Revelation interprets a time, times, and half-a-time to be $3\frac{1}{2}$ years, equivalent to 42 months with 30 days per month for a total of 1260 days; therefore, based on the book of Revelation's interpretation, a time, times, and half-a-time in Daniel 7:25 and Daniel 12:7 should be interpreted as $3\frac{1}{2}$ years of 360 days each. Esther 1:4 mentions that the king showed his splendor of riches for 180 days (one-half of 360), then in Esther 1:5 there was a feast for 7 days, (one week).

Not only is the 360-day year used in Bible prophecies; it was also used in business transactions that involved the future. In reference to the tribute paid to the Persian king Darius I, the ancient Greek historian Herodotus wrote,
"The fourth province was Cilicia. This rendered three hundred and sixty white horses, one for each day in the year, and five hundred talents of silver."[13] Herodotus also writes of the Egyptians having a calendar of twelve thirty-day months with five days added each year.[14]

Chapter 1: The 360-day future year, quotations
13. Herodotus, *The Persian Wars* II, Book III. 90, trans. by A. D. Godly, Loeb Classical Lib. 118 (Cambridge MA: Harvard Univ. Press, 1921 & 1938) p. 119
14. Herodotus, *The Persian Wars* I, Book II. 4, trans. by A. D. Godly, Loeb Classical Lib. 117 (Cambridge MA: Harvard Univ. Press, 1920 & 1926) p. 279

Chapter 2
The seventy years of Babylonian captivity and the
seventy years of desolation of the land

The seventy years of captivity in Babylon until the land
had enjoyed her Sabbath rest to fulfill seventy years is the
background to the seventy sevens prophecy told to Daniel
by the angel Gabriel.

Jeremiah 25:11-12
11 **And this whole land shall be a desolation *and* an
astonishment, and these nations shall serve the king of Babylon
seventy years.**
12 **Then it will come to pass, when seventy years are completed,
that I will punish the king of Babylon and that nation, the land
of the Chaldeans, for their iniquity, says the Lord; and I will
make it a perpetual desolation.**

Jeremiah 29:10
10 **For thus says the Lord: After seventy years are completed
at Babylon, I will visit you and perform My good word toward
you, and cause you to return to this place.**

The Lord commanded the Israelites that when you come into the land given to you, then you are to observe a Sabbath of the land and rest the land every seven years.

As described in the Torah (the law) in Leviticus 25:1-6, the children of Israel were commanded to observe a Sabbath of the land by resting the land every seven years.
Leviticus 25:1-4
1 **And the Lord spoke to Moses on Mount Sinai, saying,** 2 **"Speak to the children of Israel, and say to them: 'When you come into the land which I give you, then the land shall keep a Sabbath to the Lord.** 3 **Six years you shall sow your field, and six years you shall prune your vineyard, and gather its fruit;** 4 **but in the seventh year there shall be a Sabbath of solemn rest for the land, a Sabbath to the Lord. You shall neither sow your field nor prune your vineyard.'"**

The Northern Kingdom of Israel separated from Judah where Jerusalem is located.

After the death of Solomon in (932/931 B.C.[2:1]), Rehoboam his son reigned in his place. Northern Israel complained of the heavy tax burden they were under. The elders advised Rehoboam to listen to the people, but he took the advice of the young men and spoke of making their yoke even heaver. The people of Northern Israel said to themselves, **"What share have we in David? We have no inheritance in the son of Jesse. To your tents O Israel! Now, see to your own house, O David,"** (1 Kings 12:16).

The Northern Kingdom became idol worshipers.

Led by Jeroboam I, Northern Israel separated from Judah where the Temple was located, which was to the south. In order to keep the people of the Northern Kingdom of Israel from returning to the Temple in Judah, Jeroboam I had a gold calf built at Bethel and another at Dan and said to the people, **"It is too much for you to go up to Jerusalem. Here are your Gods, O Israel, which brought you up from the land of Egypt!"**
(1 Kings 12:28).

The people of the Northern Kingdom of Israel were taken captive and carried away to Assyria.

Hoshea, who was around the twentieth king of the Northern Kingdom of Israel did evil in the sight of the Lord. Shalmaneser, king of Assyria made Hoshea his vassal and ordered him to pay tribute. Then one year, Hoshea conspired with the king of Egypt and did not pay tribute to the king of Assyria. The king of Assyria besieged Northern Israel for three years and carried the people of Northern Israel away to Assyria and put Hoshea in prison, (2 Kings 17:1-6). The Northern Kingdom ended in (723/722 B.C.[2:2]).

Josiah, king of Judah, returned the people to the Torah (the law) and did away with idols.

Josiah, who was around the sixteenth king of Judah did right in the sight of the Lord. In the eighteenth year of his reign as workers were repairing the Temple, the high priest Hilkiah found the book of the law in the house of the Lord. Hilkiah gave the book of the law to Shaphan the scribe. Shaphan brought it to Josiah the king and read it to him. When Josiah heard the law, he tore his clothes and commanded Hilkiah, Shaphan, and others to inquire of the Lord, **"Because our fathers have not obeyed the words of this book,"** (2 Kings 22:13). They inquired of Huldah the prophetess and she told them that the Lord would bring calamity on this place and its inhabitants, but not until after Josiah. Josiah had the articles made for Baal and for Asherah taken out of the Temple and burned along with the idols in high places in the cities of Judah and took away the shrines in the high places in the cities of Samaria (the Northern Kingdom). He defiled the place called Topheth that children would not be sacrificed by fire to the Canaanite god Molech. Josiah, also commanded the people to keep the Passover and they observed a great Passover, (2 Kings 22:1-23 and 29).

Josiah was killed by an archer's arrow of the army of Pharaoh Necho I, king of Egypt, (June 25-July 23, 609 B.C.[2:3]). The people mourned and Jeremiah lamented the death of Josiah,
(2 Chronicles 35:20-26).

The kings of Judah after Josiah until the Babylonian captivity did evil in the sight of the Lord.

Jehoahaz and Jehoiakim, sons of Josiah, became kings.

The people took Jehoahaz, a son of Josiah, as king of Judah. After only three months Necho I deposed Jehoahaz and made Eliakim, another son of Josiah, king and changed his name to Jehoiakim, (2 Chronicles 36:1-4).

The Battle of Carchemish where the Babylonians and the Medes defeated the rule of the Assyrians.

At the Battle of Carchemish in (May/June, 605 B.C.[2:4]) the Babylonians, led by Nebuchadnezzar II* and the Medes, defeated the last stronghold of the Assyrians and their Egyptian allies led by Necho II that had come to help the Assyrians. Some of the Egyptian army escaped and headed south toward Egypt. The Babylonians pursued the remaining Egyptians and defeated them at Hamath.

The Babylonian army kept moving south and came to Judah where Nebuchadnezzar made Jehoiakim, king of Judah, his vassal. Nebuchadnezzar received news of his father's death and returned to Babylon to ascend the throne while leaving a major part of his army to bring captives from Judah to Babylon.

"The Babylonian chronicles mention that in the spring of the last regal year of his father, Nabopolassar (605 B.C.), Nebuchadnezzar defeated the Egyptians in two battles—the first at Carchemish, the second at Hamath. After these victories he was pursuing the enemy toward their country when he received news that his father had died on Abu 8 (Aug. 15, 605 B.C.). Thereupon he returned at once to Babylon and was crowned king on Ululu 1 (Sept. 7 605 B.C.)."[2:5]

2:5. Siegfried H. Horn and Lynn H. Wood, *The Chronology of Ezra 7,* (Washington, DC: Review and Herald Publishing Association, 1970) p. 65
See
D. J. Wiseman, *Chronicles of Chaldaean Kings (626-556)* pp. 68, 69

*In the Bible, Nebuchadnezzar, king of Babylon, sometimes spelled Nebuchadrezzar (with an 'r' in place of an 'n') in Jeremiah and Ezekiel, is referred to as Nebuchadnezzar II by modern historians.

Nebuchadnezzar II accession
Months
      Babylonian   Judah Hebrew
605 BC
5th   Abu   Ab
       Ab 8 Nabopolassar died 21st year (Aug 15, 605 B.C.)
6th   Ululu   Elul
       Elul 1 Nebuchadnezzar II crowned king (Sept. 7, 605 B.C.)
               (New Year Judah Hebrews)
7th   Tashritu   Tishri (1st year Nebuchadnezzar) Judah
8th   Arahsamnu Heshvan
9th   Kislimu   Kislev
604 BC
10th Tebetu   Tebeth
11th Shabatu   Shebat
12th Addaru   Adar
       (New Year Babylonians)
1st   Nisanu   Nisan (1st Year Nebuchadnezzar) Babylon

This chart shows the first year of Nebuchadnezzar according to those in Judah beginning in the fall on the 7th month while the first year of Nebuchadnezzar in Babylon began later in the spring on the 1st month, so the counting of the year of Nebuchadnezzar in Judah began six months earlier than in Babylon.

The Bible speaks of Jehoiakim becoming a vassal of Nebuchadnezzar while remaining as king of Judah; whereas Daniel was taken captive to Babylon.

In the third year of Jehoiakim as king of Judah, (605 BC.[2:6]) Nebuchadnezzar, king of Babylon, made Jehoiakim his vassal and instructed the master of his eunuchs that some of the gifted young men and descendants of the king be brought to Babylon. Daniel and his three companions were among the young men chosen to serve the king of Babylon, (Daniel 1:1-4).

Daniel used the seventh month, the month of Tishri as the New Year in counting the third year of Jehoiakim, king of Judah.

Jeremiah 46:1-2
1 The word of the LORD which came to Jeremiah the prophet against the nations. 2 Against Egypt. Concerning the army of pharaoh Necho king of Egypt, which was by the River Euphrates in Carchemish, and which Nebuchadnezzar king of Babylon defeated in the fourth year of Jehoiakim the son of Josiah, king of Judah.

Jeremiah prophesied that the defeat of the Egyptians by the Babylonians was a judgment against Egypt. Jeremiah dates the Battle of Carchemish, which happened in 605 B.C. as happening in the fourth year of Jehoiakim, whereas, Daniel dates that same summer as the third year of Jehoiakim.

Jehoiakim became king in the fall of 609 B.C. after the seventh month. If Jeremiah was using the first month in the spring for counting the year of the king, then each summer Jeremiah's year of the king would be one year greater than Daniel's year of the king. The reason for Jeremiah using the first month may have been because he was prophesying against Egypt and Babylon that used the first month for counting the year of the king.

Jeremiah dictated the words of the Lord as Baruch wrote the words onto a scroll.

In the fourth year of Jehoiakim as king of Judah (605 B.C. by Jeremiah's way of counting), this word came to the prophet Jeremiah that he write on a scroll all the words concerning Israel, Judah and other nations the Lord had spoken to him beginning in the reign of Josiah. So Jeremiah asked Baruch to write on the scroll the words of the Lord as Jeremiah dictated them to him. Since Jeremiah was confined, he asked Baruch to read the scroll in the house of the Lord, (Jeremiah 36:1-6).

Baruch read the scroll near a gate of the temple.

In the ninth month of the fifth year of Jehoiakim at a fast to the Lord, Baruch read the words of the scroll in the upper court at the entry of the New Gate of the Lord's house, in the hearing of all the people. (Jeremiah 36:9-10).

Jeremiah prophesied seventy years of captivity in
Babylon that the land may be desolate seventy years.

The prophet Jeremiah spoke against the sin they had committed since they entered the land God had given them. They were keeping idols in high places in the hills and under every green tree and worshiping them. They had not kept the Sabbath of the land by resting the land every seven years. Because they had not observed seventy Sabbaths of the land, they would go into captivity so the land could be desolate for seventy years of rest.

Jeremiah 25:11-12
11 **And this whole land shall be a desolation *and* an astonishment, and these nations shall serve the king of Babylon seventy years.**
12 **Then it will come to pass, when seventy years are completed, *that* I will punish the king of Babylon and that nation, the land of the Chaldeans, for their iniquity, says the Lord; and I will make it a perpetual desolation.**
Jeremiah 29:10
10 **For thus says the Lord: After seventy years are completed at Babylon, I will visit you and perform My good word toward you, and cause you to return to this place.**

Officials heard the words of the scroll and brought the
scroll to Jehoiakim, king of Judah, and read it to him.

Whenever three or four columns of the scroll were read to Jehoiakim, he cut them off with a scribe's knife and threw them into the fire, (Jeremiah 36:20-23).

Then the word of the Lord came to Jeremiah to take a scroll and write all the words of the first scroll on it. As Jeremiah dictated, Baruch wrote on the scroll all the words Jehoiakim had burned in the fire and many similar words were added, (Jeremiah 36:27-32).

Jehoiakim paid tribute to Nebuchadnezzar three years and then rebelled. After that Judah was raided by bands of neighboring nations. Jehoiakim reigned eleven years. Jehoiakim was killed (Dec. 9, 598 or Jan. 16, 597 B.C.[2:7]) fulfilling Jeremiah's prophecy, **"His dead body shall be cast out to the heat of the day and the frost of the night,"** (Jeremiah 36:30).

Jehoiachin son of Jehoiakim became king.

Jehoiachin became king after the death of his father, Jehoiakim. At that time Nebuchadnezzar's army was besieging Jerusalem and Nebuchadnezzar came against Jerusalem, (2 Kings 24:8-12).

2 Kings 24:12

12 Then Jehoiachin king of Judah, his mother, his servants, his princes, and his officers went out to the king of Babylon; and the king of Babylon, in the eighth year of his reign, took him prisoner.

The Babylonian chronicles says that on Addaru 2 of the 7th year, Nebuchadnezzar captured Jerusalem and deposed the king.

Months

	Babylonian	Judah Hebrews
598 BC.		
	(New Year Babylonians 7th year of Nebuchadnezzar)	
1st	Nisanu	Nisan
2nd	Aiaru	Iyyar
3rd	Simanu	Sivan
4th	Duzu	Tammuz
5th	Abu	Ab
6th	Ululu	Elul
	(New Year Hebrews 8th year of Nebuchadnezzar in Judah)	
7th	Ululu II	Tishri
8th	Tashritu	Heshvan
9th	Arahsamnu	Kislev
10th	Kislimu	Tebeth
597 BC		
11th	Tebetu	Shebat
12th	Shabatu	Adar I
13th	Addaru	Adar II

In his 7th year (which was a 13-month year), Nebuchadnezzar took Jehoiachin prisoner and captured Jerusalem on the 2nd day of the month of Addaru (Babylonian) (March 16, 597 B.C.[2:8]), which was the 8th year of Nebuchadnezzar (Judah).

A month later on Nisan 10 Jehoiachin and the prophet Ezekiel were carried away to Babylon (April 22, 597 B.C.[2:9]).

Jehoiachin reigned three months as king of Judah and he was taken prisoner on Addaru 2 in the seventh year of Nebuchadnezzar according to the Babylonian way of counting the first month, the month of Nisanu as the New Year (March 16, 597 B.C.). The eighth year according to the Bible's book of Kings way of counting the seventh month, the month of Tishri as the New Year.

Nebuchadnezzar carried away many treasures from the house of the Lord and took ten thousand men captive to Babylon, (2 Kings 24:13-16).

Jehoiachin was exiled to Babylon on Nisan 10 in the eighth year of Nebuchadnezzar (April 22, 597 B.C.). Ezekiel was among those taken captive to Babylon at that time. The date of the exile of Jehoiachin to Babylon is important because it is used as a reference date by Ezekiel to date several events during the Babylonian captivity.

Nebuchadnezzar made Zedekiah king.

Nebuchadnezzar, king of Babylon, made Mattaniah, king of Judah, and changed his name to Zedekiah. Jeremiah 51:59 speaks of Zedekiah going to Babylon in the fourth year of his reign; apparently, he was summoned to appear there and then, returned to Judah. He reigned eleven years in Jerusalem. He rebelled against Nebuchadnezzar and then in the ninth year, in the tenth month on the tenth day of the month (Jan. 15, 588 B.C.[2:10]), Nebuchadnezzar and his army came against Jerusalem (2 Kings 24:17-20 and 25:1).

Jeremiah asked Seraiah in the fourth year of Zedekiah to take a scroll with his words to Babylon.

Jeremiah 51:59-64

59 The word which Jeremiah the prophet commanded Seraiah, the son of Neriah, the son of Mahseiah, when he went with Zedekiah the king of Judah to Babylon in the fourth year of his reign. And Seraiah *was* the quartermaster. 60 So Jeremiah wrote in a book all the evil that would come upon Babylon, all these words that are written against Babylon. 61 And Jeremiah said to Seraiah, "When you arrive in Babylon and see it, and read all these words. 62 then you shall say, 'O Lord, You have spoken against this place to cut it off, so that none shall remain

**in it, neither man nor beast, but it shall be desolate forever.' 63
Now it shall be, when you had finished reading this book** *that*
**you shall tie a stone to it and throw it out into the Euphrates.
64 Then you shall say, 'Thus Babylon shall sink and not rise
from the catastrophe that I will bring upon her. And they shall
be weary.'" Thus far are the words of Jeremiah.**

Jer. 51:59-64 is a very important passage that explains how the scroll with the words dictated by Jeremiah to Baruch got to Babylon where Daniel was a captive of Nebuchadnezzar, king of Babylon. Seraiah, who may have been the brother of Baruch, was told by Jeremiah to read the scroll condemning Babylon and then to tie a rock to it and throw it into the Euphrates, but instead it was preserved in Babylon.

The notation, **"Thus far are the words of Jeremiah"** that is in the present book of Jeremiah in the Old Testament indicates that the scroll that Jeremiah asked Seraiah to bring to Babylon is the same book of Jeremiah we have in the Old Testament. The words of Jeremiah dictated to Baruch that are in the Old Testament contain a considerable amount of condemnation against Babylon. Seraiah brought the scroll with the words of Jeremiah to Babylon in the fourth year of Zedekiah (about 593 B.C.).

Daniel 9:1-2
**1 In the first year of Darius the son of Ahasuerus, of the lineage of
the Medes, who was made king over the realm of the Chaldeans— 2
in the first year of his reign I, Daniel, understood by the books the
number of the years** *specified* **by the word of the Lord through
Jeremiah the prophet that He would accomplish seventy years in the
desolations of Jerusalem.**

The exact time of the reign of Darius the Mede has not been determined; however, in Daniel 6:28 he is mentioned before Cyrus. Daniel had read the words of the prophet Jeremiah and he began to wonder what would happen after the seventy years of desolation of the land. During the first year of Darius the Mede, while Daniel was praying to the Lord God, in answer to Daniel's prayer, the angel Gabriel was sent to Daniel and the angel Gabriel told Daniel the seventy sevens prophecy.

The beginning of the Babylonian Captivity needed to occur before the beginning of the desolation of the land prophesied by Jeremiah.

While he was captive in Babylon, Ezekiel spoke the word of the Lord and marked the day of the siege of Jerusalem that began the seventy years of desolation of the land.

Ezekiel 24:1-2
1 **Again in the ninth year, in the tenth month, on the tenth** *day* **of the month, the word of the Lord came to me, saying,**
2 **"Son of man, write down the name of the day, this very day —the king of Babylon started his siege against Jerusalem this very day."**

The beginning of the desolation began with the siege of Jerusalem when the people had been taken off the land and Nebuchadnezzar's army had surrounded the city and animals could not be brought in to sacrifice in the Temple. The word of the Lord came to Ezekiel, saying, **"Write down this day."**

When Ezekiel says, **"In the ninth year,"** he is referring to the ninth year of captivity of Jehoiachin and himself. "The ninth year of exile of Jehoiachin was 589/588 B.C. The tenth month is Tebeth (Dec/Jan), and in 588 B.C. the tenth day of Tebeth was Jan. 15, 588 B.C."[2:11]

Nebuchadnezzar's army besieged Jerusalem and they breeched the wall.

Nebuchadnezzar's army besieged Jerusalem until it fell in the eleventh year of Zedekiah on the ninth day in the fourth month (July 18, 586 B.C.[2:12]) (2 Kings 25:2-3).

2 Chronicles 36:20-21
20 **And those who escaped from the sword he carried away to Babylon, where they became servants to him and his sons until the rule of the kingdom of Persia,** 21 **to fulfill the word of the Lord by the mouth of Jeremiah, until the land had enjoyed her Sabbaths. As long as she lay desolate she kept Sabbath, to fulfill seventy years.**

The prophecy was for seventy years of captivity in Babylon until the seventy years of desolation of the land; so the land could enjoy her Sabbaths to fulfill seventy years. Notice that what is fulfilled is the seventy years of rest of the land.

The captain of the guard of Nebuchadnezzar's army led the destruction of Jerusalem and the temple.

2 Kings 25:8-10
8 And in the fifth month, on the seventh day of the month (which was the nineteenth year of king Nebuchadnezzar king of Babylon), Nebuzaradan the captain of the guard, a servant of the king of Babylon, came to Jerusalem. 9 He burned the house of the Lord and the king's house; all the houses of Jerusalem, that is, all the houses of the great, he burned with fire. 10 And all the army of the Chaldeans who *were with* the captain of the guard broke down the walls of Jerusalem all around.

The nineteenth year of Nebuchadnezzar, (using Tishri for counting the year of the king as per Judah) and the fifth month is (Aug. 586 B.C.). The seventh day as per 2 Kings 25:8 would be (Aug 14, 586 B.C.) and the tenth day as per Jer. 52:12 would be (Aug. 17, 586 B.C.).[2:13]

The wall of Jerusalem was torn down in 586 B.C. and it was not repaired again until Artaxerxes I gave Nehemiah letters in 444 BC. giving him authority and providing for materials to rebuild the wall, which was a span of 142 Julian years without a wall.

During the 1970s, Israeli archaeologist Nahman Avigad led an excavation in the Jewish Old City part of Jerusalem that uncovered some remains of Hezekiah's Broad Wall that had been mostly torn down by the army of Nebuchadnezzar in 586 B.C. The Broad Wall was originally eight meters high.

Concrete walls were built bordering the excavation with an iron fence at street level surrounding the excavation.

Excavation showing remains of Hezekiah's Broad Wall

Picture of diagram showing Hezekiah's Broad Wall placed on the wall of the excavation in the Old City Jewish part of Jerusalem

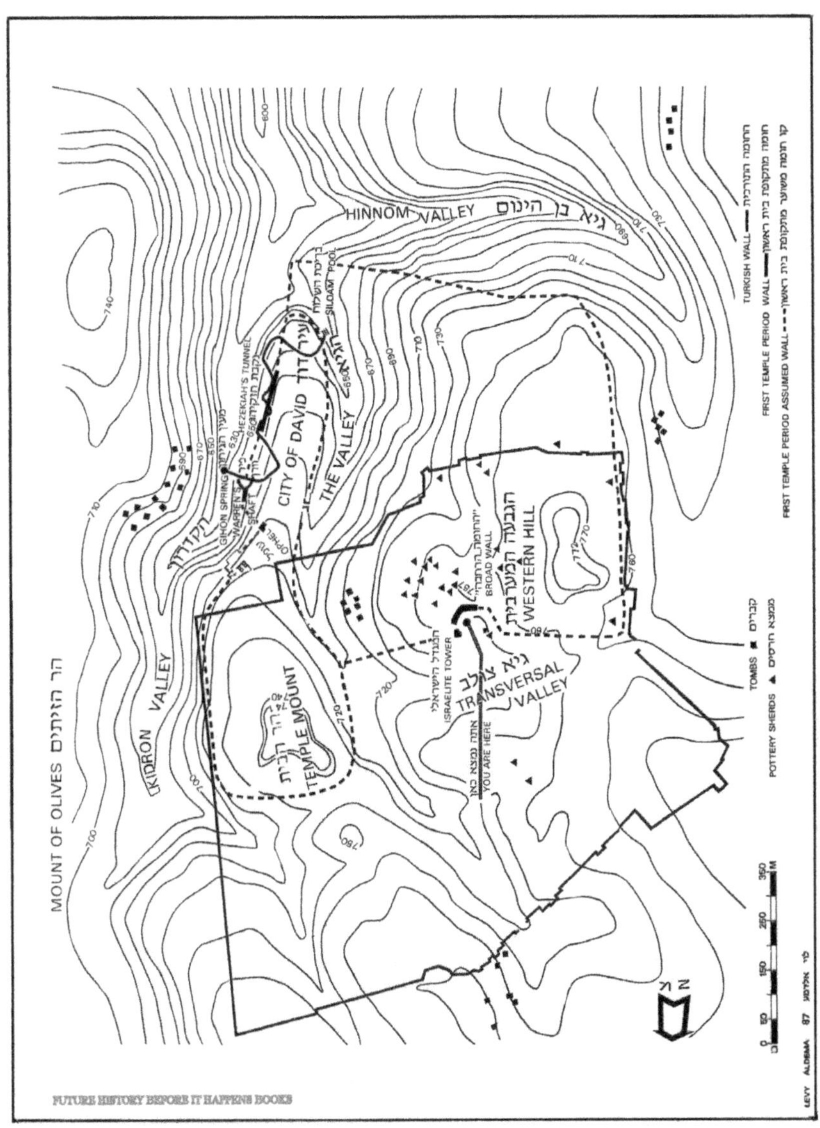

"YOU ARE HERE," points to the location of the Broad Wall excavation.
The segmented line shows, "FIRST TEMPLE PERIOD ASSUMED WALL."
The solid line above where it says, "CITY OF DAVID" shows a segment of "FIRST TEMPLE PERIOD WALL."
The long solid line shows, "TURKISH WALL" that was built up (some of it upon previous walls) by the Muslim Turks that still remains in modern Jerusalem.

In the first year of his reign (over Babylon), Cyrus the Great, king of Persia, released Israelites to rebuild the temple at Jerusalem before the seventy years of desolation of the land were over.

In a prophecy in Isaiah 44:28 the Lord speaks of Cyrus as his shepherd [anointed one] and credits him with the rebuilding of Jerusalem and the laying of the foundation of the temple.

Isaiah 44:28
28 Who says of Cyrus, '*He is* My shepherd, and he shall perform all My pleasure, Saying to Jerusalem, "You shall be built," and to the temple, "Your foundation shall be laid."'

Considering that Cyrus was made aware of the prophecy in Isaiah 44:28 explains why Cyrus speaks of the Lord God of heaven commanding him (Cyrus) to build Him (the Lord God of heaven) a house at Jerusalem which is in Judah.

2 Chronicles 36:22-23
22 Now the first year of Cyrus king of Persia, that the word of the Lord by the mouth of Jeremiah might be fulfilled, the Lord stirred up the spirit of Cyrus king of Persia, so that he made a proclamation throughout all his kingdom, and also *put it* in writing saying,
23 Thus says Cyrus king of Persia: All the kingdoms of the earth the Lord God of heaven has given me. And He has commanded me to build Him a house at Jerusalem which *is* in Judah. Who *is* among you of all His people? May the Lord his God *be* with him, and let him go up!

In 2 Chronicles 36:22, **"that the word of the Lord by the mouth of Jeremiah might be fulfilled"** refers to the prophecy in Jeremiah 29:10 that they would return to the land after the seventy years of captivity in Babylon. Jeremiah also speaks of rising early and prophesying to the people. Not everyone returned in the first year of Cyrus (538/537 B.C.[2:14]). Instead, the return of the captives happened in stages. The return in the first year of Cyrus was before the seventy years of desolation of the land were completed.

Even though they had been released in the first year of Cyrus, they were still unclean because the seventy years of rest of the land had not been completed.

Those that had returned to Judah had been working on their own houses so the Lord sent Haggai to remind them that it was time to rebuild the Temple. According to Haggai 1:1-8, in the second year of the king Darius, on the first day of the sixth month, (August 29, 520 B.C.[2:15]) Haggai the prophet spoke the word of the LORD to the governor of Judah and the high priest that now was the time to build the temple, saying that they should go into the mountains and bring wood to build the Temple.

Then according to Haggai 2:15-19, three months later after the foundation of the temple was laid in the second year of the king Darius, on the twenty-fourth day of the ninth month, (December 18, 520 B.C.) (see p. 38) the LORD spoke to the prophet Haggai saying that he should ask the priests a question concerning the law. Haggai 2:10-19

10 On the twenty-fourth *day* of the ninth *month*, in the second year of Darius, the word of the LORD came by Haggai the prophet, saying,

11 "Thus says the LORD of hosts: 'Now ask the priests *concerning the* law, saying,

12 "If one carries holy meat in the fold of his garment, and with the edge he touches bread or stew, wine or oil, or any food, will it become holy?"' Then the priests answered and said "No."

13 And Haggai said, "If *one who is* unclean *because* of a dead body touches any of these, will it be unclean?" So the priest answered and said, "It shall be unclean."

14 Then Haggai answered and said, '"So is this people, and so is this nation before Me,' says the LORD, 'And so is the work of their hands; and what they offer there is unclean.

15 And now, carefully consider from this day forward: from before stone was laid upon stone in the temple of the Lord—

16 since those *days*, when *one* came to a heap of twenty ephahs, there were *but* ten; when *one* came to the wine vat to draw out fifty baths from the press, there were *but* twenty.

**17 I struck you with blight and mildew and hail in all the labors of your hands; yet you did not *turn* to me,' says the Lord.
18 'Consider now from this day forward, from the twenty-fourth day of the ninth month, from the day that the foundation of the LORD'S temple was laid—consider it:
19 Is the seed still in the barn? As yet the vine, the fig tree, the pomegranate, and the olive tree have not yielded *fruit*. But from this day I will bless you.'"**

Haggai asked a priest a riddle to demonstrate that even though they had been released by Cyrus they were still unclean and the land refused to give good crops because the land was resting until the seventy years were over.

Haggai asked the priest, "If there is holy meat in the fold of a garment and the garment touches food does that make the food holy?" The priests answered, "No." Then Haggai asked the priests, "If an unclean person touches food does that make the food unclean?" The priests answered, "It shall be unclean."

Then Haggai said, **"'So is this people, and so is this nation before Me,' says the LORD, 'And so is the work of their hands; and what they offer there is unclean,'"** (Haggai 2:14). The riddle that Haggai asked the priests had an application concerning the end of the seventy years of desolation prophesied by Jeremiah. Just as the meat in the fold of the garment did not make the food the garment touched holy, likewise, the edict of Cyrus that released some of the captives in Babylon before the seventy years of desolation were over in order to lay the foundation of the Temple did not make them holy for they were still unclean.

The prophet Haggai told the people of Judah after they laid the foundation of the temple that the seventy years of desolation were over and he pronounced the word of the Lord blessing them from that day.

Then after Haggai had told the people that they were still unclean before the LORD, he pronounced a blessing on them that coincided with the end of the seventy years of desolation prophesied by Jeremiah and the laying of the foundation of the

Temple. Speaking the word of the Lord, Haggai said, **"Consider now from this day forward, from the twenty-fourth day of the ninth month, from the day that the foundation of the LORD'S temple was laid—consider it:…from this day I will bless you,"** (Haggai 2:18 and 19c).

Darius I, king of Persia, punished the Babylonians in fulfilment of Jeremiah's prophecy.

Jeremiah 25:12

12 'Then it will come to pass, when seventy years are completed, *that* I will punish the king of Babylon and that nation, the land of the Chaldeans, for their iniquity,' says the Lord; 'and I will make it a perpetual desolation.'

Jeremiah prophesied saying that when the seventy years are completed the Babylonians will be punished. After the foundation of the temple was laid, the prophet Haggai blessed the Hebrews of Judah on the twenty fourth day of the ninth month, the month of Kislev, in the second year of Darius I because the land had finished its sabbath rest.

The Greek historian, Herodotus, speaks of the punishment of Babylon by Darius I after their second rebellion at a time in agreement with the prophet Haggai.

"Thus was Babylon the second time taken. Having mastered the Babylonians, Darius destroyed their walls and reft away all their gates, neither of which things Cyrus had done at the first taking of Babylon; moreover he impaled about three thousand men that were chief among them; as for the rest, he gave them back their city to dwell in."[2:16]

2:16. Herodotus, *The Persian Wars* II, Book III. 159, trans. by A. D. Godly, Loeb Classical Library 118 (Cambridge, MA: Harvard University Press, 1921 revised 1938) pp. 193 & 195.

The punishment of Babylon by Darius I and not by Cyrus, shows that Jeremiah's prophecy was fulfilled in the time of Darius I, not in the time of Cyrus. That is confirmed by an extrabiblical source, the ancient Greek historian, Herodotus.

Ezra 6:15 gives the date when the rebuilding of the temple was completed.

Ezra 6:15
15 **Now the temple was finished on the third day of the month Adar, which was in the sixth year of the reign of king Darius.** (March 12, 515 B.C.[2:17])

After the Babylonian Captivity, those that returned had learned to listen to the prophets and not worship idols.

During the years of captivity in Babylon, the captives saw the hopelessness of idol worship firsthand and they realized they had so much more in the Lord. During the Babylonian Captivity was a time when the prophets prophesied many things about the future.

Ezekiel 36:24-27
24. **For I will take you from among the nations, gather you out of all countries, and bring you into your own land. 25 Then I will sprinkle clean water on you, and you shall be clean; I will cleanse you from all your filthiness and from all your idols. 26 I will give you a new heart and put a new spirit within you; I will take the heart of stone out of your flesh and give you a heart of flesh. 27 I will put My spirit within you and cause you to walk in My statutes, and you will keep My judgments and do *them*.**

The prophecy in Ezekiel 36:26-27 that says, "**I will put My spirit within you**" rises to Christian conversion with born-again Christians having the indwelling of the Holy Spirit within them.

The prophet Ezekiel marked the beginning of the seventy years of desolation of the land and the prophet Haggai marked the end of the seventy years of desolation of the land.

In Ezekiel 24:1-2 the prophet Ezekiel speaks of the beginning of the siege of Jerusalem when the people had been taken off the land. The day Ezekiel says to write down is **the ninth year, in the tenth month, on the tenth *day* of the month,**

When Ezekiel says, **"In the ninth year,"** he is referring to the ninth year of captivity of Jehoiachin and himself, "The ninth year of exile of Jehoiachin was 589/588. The tenth month is Tebeth. (Dec/Jan), and in 588 B.C. the tenth day of Tebeth was (Jan. 15, 588 B.C. Julian)."[2:18]

The prophet Haggai says, **"Consider now from this day."** It is the second year of the Persian king Darius I on the twenty fourth day of the sixth month. The second year of Darius I is 520 B.C. on the Julian calendar. The ninth month on the Hebrew calendar is Kislev. In 520 B.C. Julian, the first day in the month of Kislev was Nov. 25, 520 B.C.[2:19] Then calculating to the twenty fourth day of Kislev in 520 B.C. would be Dec 18, 520 B.C. Julian.

The seventy years of desolation needs to be calculated on a lunar calendar with 360 days in a year.

In those days the ancient Babylonians and Hebrews used a lunar calendar. Each time there was a new crescent moon that indicated the beginning of a new month. When they thought of a year in the future, they thought of an ideal lunar year of 360 days.

In reference to the tribute paid to the Persian king Darius I, the ancient Greek historian Herodotus wrote:

"The fourth province was Cilicia. This rendered three hundred and sixty white horses, one for each day in the year, and five hundred talents of silver."[2:20]

2:20. Herodotus, *The Persian Wars* II, Bk. III. 90, trans. by A. D. Godly, Loeb Classical Library 118 (Cambridge, MA: Harvard Univ. Press, 1938) p. 119

With the desolation of the land, the land rested seventy 360-day lunar years.

From January 588 to December 520 is a span of 69 Julian years. Multiplying 69 Julian years times 365.25 days per Julian solar year equals 25,202.25 Julian solar days. Then, 25,202.25 Julian solar days divided by 360 days per lunar year equals 70 lunar years of 360 days each.

Jerusalem was without a temple for seventy years.

The destruction of the temple, Aug. 17, 586 B.C. (see page 32) minus the rebuilt temple finished, Mar. 12, 515 B.C. (see page 40) equals 70 Julian years and 7 months.

Chapter 2: The seventy years of Babylonian captivity and the seventy years of desolation of the land, quotations.

2:1. Jack Finegan, *Handbook of Biblical Chronology* (Hendrickson Publishers Inc.; Peabody, MA., 1999), p. 249 § 424   932/931 B.C. (death of Solomon).

2:2. Ibid., p. 250 § 426   723/722 B.C. (Northern kingdom ended).

2:3. Ibid., p. 252 § 430   June 25-July 23, 609 B.C. (Josiah killed by arrow).

2:4. Ibid., p. 254 § 433   May/June, 605 B.C. (Battle Carchemish).

2:5. Siegfried H. Horn and Lynn H. Wood, *The Chronology of Ezra 7,* (Washington, DC: Review and Herald Publishing Association, 1970) p. 65 (Sept. 7 605 B.C. (Nebuchadnezzar crowned king of Babylon).

See D. J. Wiseman, *Chronicles of Chaldaean Kings (626-556)* pp 68, 69.

2:6. Finegan, *Handbook of Biblical Chronology*, p. 254 § 433   605 B.C. (Jehoiakim a vassal of Nebuchadnezzar; Daniel taken captive to Babylon).

2:7. Ibid., p. 257 § 440   Dec. 9, 598 or Jan. 597 B.C.   (Jehoiakim killed).

2:8. Horn and Wood, *The Chronology of Ezra 7*, p. 65   March 16, 597 B.C. (Jehoiachin surrendered to Nebuchadnezzar and Jerusalem captured).

2:9. Finegan, *Handbook of Biblical Chronology*, p. 257 § 440 and p. 262 § 447 Nisan 10, Hebrew; April 22, 597 B.C. (Jehoiakin & Ezekiel exiled to Babylon).

2:10. Ibid., p. 259 § 442   Jan. 15, 588 B.C. (Neb. came against Jerusalem).

2:11. Ibid., p. 259 § 442 Jan. 15, 588 B.C. (Ezekiel, **"Write down this day"**).

2:12. Ibid., p. 265 § 451   July 18, 586 BC. (Jerusalem wall was breached).

2:13. Ibid., p. 259 § 443 8/14 or 17, 586 B.C. (Jerusalem & temple destroyed).

2:14. Ibid., p. 266 § 454   538/537 B.C. (Cyrus released captives).

2:15. Ibid., p. 267 § 457   8/29, 520 B.C., Haggai exhorted, "Build the temple"

2:16. Herodotus, *The Persian Wars* II, Bk. III 159, trans. by A. D. Godly, Loeb Classical Library 118 (Cambridge, MA: Harvard University Press 1921 rev. 1938) pp. 193 & 195 (Babylon punished by Darius I, which Cyrus had not done).

2:17. Finegan, *Handbook of Biblical Chronology*, p. 267 § 457

2:18. Ibid., p. 265 § 451   Jan. 15, 588 B.C. (Ezekiel, **"Write down this day"**).

2:19. Richard A. Parker and Waldo H. Dubberstein, *Babylonian Chronology 620 B.C.-A.D. 75* (Eugene, OR: Wipf and Stock Publishers, 2007) p. 30 (Previously Published by Brown University Press, 1956.

(Dec. 18, 520 B.C., Foundation of the temple was laid coinciding with the 70 years of sabbath rest of the land).

2:20. Herodotus, *The Persian Wars* II, Bk. III. 90, trans. by A. D. Godly, Loeb Classical Library 118 (Cambridge, MA: Harvard University Press, 1938), 119

PP. 33 & 34 Broad Wall, photographed in Jerusalem by Douglas Ophus

P. 35 Broad Wall Diagram, photographed in Jerusalem by Jason Ophus. Then the brown background of the diagram was clarified using Corel Paint Shop Pro 2018 eraser tool by Douglas Ophus and printed in grayscale.

Chapter 3

The seventy sevens prophecy told to Daniel by the angel Gabriel (Dan. 9:1-3 and 9:24-27)

Daniel became a captive of Nebuchadnezzar, king of Babylon.

At the Battle of Carchemish in the spring of 605 B.C., the Babylonians and the Medes led by Nebuchadnezzar II defeated the last stronghold of the Assyrians led by Ashur-uballit II and their Egyptian ally led by Necho II the son of Necho I who remained in Egypt. Nebuchadnezzar pursued some retreating Egyptians and defeated them again at Hamath. Nebuchadnezzar came to Judah and made Jehoiakim his vassal.

Nebuchadnezzar received news his father had died; he returned to Babylon to ascend to his father's throne, but he left behind a substantial part of the army to take captives.

Daniel was among the earliest group of captives taken to Babylon; he was among a special group of young men taken captive to Babylon.

Daniel 1:1-2 says that in the third year of Jehoiakim, king of Judah, (605 B.C.) Nebuchadnezzar, king of Babylon, besieged Jerusalem and Jehoiakim was delivered into his hands. That would have been after the Battle of Carchemish in the spring of 605 B.C., but before Nebuchadnezzar received news of his father death and returned to Babylon to ascend to his father's throne on September 7, 605 B.C.

Daniel 1:3-5 says that the master of the eunuchs was instructed to bring some of the descendants of the king, some nobles, and young men gifted in wisdom and quick to understand to serve in the king's palace. Jeremiah dictated another scroll to the scribe Baruch after Jehoiakim burned the first one in the fire and Jeremiah added many more words. Jeremiah's scroll was still being written during the time Daniel was captive in Babylon. Daniel says that he had been reading the prophet Jeremiah. For Daniel to be reading the prophet Jeremiah while he was in Babylon would require that the scroll Daniel was reading was brought to Babylon from Jerusalem. In Jeremiah 51:59-64, Jeremiah asked Seraiah when he went to Babylon in the fourth year of Zedekiah to take a scroll with his words to Babylon.

Daniel prayed asking the Lord God what would happen after the seventy years of the desolation of Jerusalem.

Daniel 9: 1-3
1 In the first year of Darius the son of Ahasuerus, of the lineage of the Medes, who was made king over the realm of the Chaldeans.
2 In the first year of his reign* I, Daniel understood by the books the number of the years *specified* by the word of the Lord through Jeremiah the prophet, that He would accomplish seventy years in the desolations of Jerusalem.
3 Then I set my face toward the Lord God to make request by prayer and supplications, with fasting, sackcloth, and ashes.
New King James Version (Nashville: Thomas Nelson Inc., 1982)

*** (*over Babylon*)**

While Daniel was praying, the angel Gabriel appeared to him.

Daniel 9:20-24
20 While I was speaking and praying, confessing my sin and the sin of my people Israel and making my request to the Lord my God for his holy hill—
21 while I was still in prayer, Gabriel, the man I had seen in the earlier vision, came to me in swift flight about the time of the evening sacrifice.
22 He instructed me and said to me, "Daniel I have now come to give you insight and understanding.
23 As soon as you began to pray, an answer was given, which I have come to tell you, for you are highly esteemed. Therefore, consider the message and understand the vision:
24 "Seventy sevens are decreed for your people and your holy city to finish transgression, to put an end to sin, to atone for wickedness, to bring in everlasting righteousness, to seal up vision and prophecy and to anoint the most holy."
Interlinear NIV Hebrew-English Old Testament, John R. Kohlenberger III,
(Grand Rapids: Zondervan Publishing House, 1987)

25 "Know therefore and understand, *that* from the going forth of the command to restore and build Jerusalem until Messiah the Prince, *there shall be* seven weeks, and sixty-two weeks;

The street shall be built again, and the wall, even in troublesome times.

26 And after the sixty-two weeks Messiah shall be cut off, but not for Himself; and the people of the prince who *is* to come shall destroy the city and the sanctuary. The end of it *shall be* with a flood.

New King James Version (Nashville: Thomas Nelson Inc., 1982)

26c War will continue until the end, and desolations have been decreed.

27 He will confirm a covenant with many for one seven. In the middle of the seven, he will put an end to sacrifice and offering. And on a wing (*of the temple*) he will set up an abomination that causes desolation, until the end that is decreed is poured out on him."

(*Interlinear NIV Hebrew-English Old Testament,* John R. Kohlenberger III, (Grand Rapids: Zondervan Publishing House, 1987)

Chapter 4

The preface to the counting of the seventy sevens that speaks of the work of the Messiah for the people (Daniel 9:24)

Daniel 9:24 is a preface to the counting of the seventy sevens in the seventy sevens prophecy; it speaks of several lofty things to be accomplished during the time of the seventy sevens.

In the preface to the counting of the seventy sevens there are six infinitive phrases, which begin with "to." They are things that pertain to the accomplishment of the Messiah who was cut off, but not for Himself; He was cut off for the people. They are all positive accomplishments that are aspects of the work of the Messiah.

Daniel 9:24

24 "Seventy sevens are decreed for your people and your holy city to finish transgression, to put an end to sin, to atone for wickedness, to bring in everlasting righteousness, to seal up vision and prophecy and to anoint the most holy."
The interlinear NIV Heb. Eng. O. T.; John R. Kohlenberger III (Zondervan)

The scriptural background for these things may be explained by referring to the offerings mentioned in Leviticus and the offerings personified as being fulfilled by a person being the offering in Isaiah chapter 53.

In the seventy sevens prophecy there is a further connection between the personified offerings as being fulfilled by a person being the offering in Isaiah and the Messiah, the ruler in the seventy sevens prophecy. The seventy sevens prophecy describes how the Messiah is going to accomplish the personified offerings as being fulfilled by a person being the offering mentioned in Isaiah. He is going to be cut off, but not for Himself. He is going to be cut off for the people.

The preface to the counting of the seventy sevens details certain aspects of the accomplishments of the Messiah.

Then, lo and behold their fulfilment is described in the New Testament!

The order of the offerings in Leviticus is from the Godward aspect.

"The order of the offerings in Leviticus is from the Godward Aspect."[4:1] In order they are: the burnt offering 1:1-17, the meal offering 2:1-16, the peace offering 3:1-17, the sin offering 4:1-5:14, and the trespass offering 5:14-6:7.

The manward aspect of the offerings begins with the trespass offering; when a sinner would give an offering, he would begin with the trespass offering.

The Levitical offerings are personified as a person being the offering in Isaiah

The Levitical offerings are personified as being fulfilled by a person being the offering in Isaiah beginning in the direction of a sinner seeking forgiveness; although, it repeats the order at times, some of them are as follows:

Isa. 53:5 **But He *was* wounded for our <u>transgressions</u>, He was bruised for our <u>iniquities</u>; The chastisement for our <u>peace</u> was upon Him, And by His stripes we are <u>healed</u>.**

Isa. 53:6b **And the Lord has laid on Him the <u>iniquity</u> of us all.**

Isa. 53:8b **For He was cut off from the land of the living; For the <u>transgressions</u> of My people He was stricken.**

Isa. 53:10a **When you made His soul an <u>offering for sin</u>.**

Isa. 53:11b **By His knowledge My righteous Servant shall <u>justify</u> many, For He shall bear their <u>iniquities</u>.**

Isa. 53:12b **Because He <u>poured out his soul</u> onto death, And He was numbered with transgressors, And He <u>bore the sin</u> of many, And made intercession for the <u>transgressors</u>.**

In Daniel 9:24 the preface to the counting of the seventy sevens, the Levitical offerings are fulfilled in the manward direction.

In the preface to the counting of the seventy sevens, the Levitical offerings are fulfilled to the direction of a sinner seeking forgiveness, culminating with the anointing of the Most Holy who made it all possible, since the Godward aspect begins with the Most Holy. The preface to the counting of the seventy sevens details certain aspects of the accomplishments of the Messiah.

→**Seventy sevens are decreed**

The Lord God honored Daniel's prayer and sent the angel Gabriel to tell him a prophecy of seventy-sevens. Jeremiah's prophecy of the desolation of the land with the seventy years of captivity in Babylon is the overall context for the Seventy Sevens prophecy brought by Gabriel to Daniel. Since Jeremiah's prophecy was for seventy years; the Seventy Sevens prophecy that Gabriel told to Daniel is also understood to be in years. The Hebrew word שָׁבֻעִים [4:2] 'sevens' that is in the Seventy Sevens prophecy is a plural form of the Hebrew word for seven. It has the concept of a group of seven. It is often translated as weeks as in the feast of weeks. Dan. 10:2 speaks of three sevens of days, which has traditionally been translated as three weeks of days, and Dan. 10:3 also speaks of three sevens of days, which has traditionally been translated as three weeks of days. For many centuries the seventy sevens prophecy has been translated in English Bibles as seventy weeks. However, it is better to translate it in the Bible as seventy sevens in the first place and avoid using the confusing term seventy weeks of years that many commentaries have found necessary to do in order to explain Bible translations with seventy weeks. The prophecy is for seventy groups of seven years. There are three groups of sevens that need to be treated separately. They are: seven sevens, sixty-two sevens, and one seven.

→**For your people and your holy city**

This prophecy prophesies that Jerusalem will be rebuilt with streets and a wall, and then prophesies that Jerusalem and the Temple will be destroyed again, which we now know was accomplished by the Roman army in 70 A.D. The accomplishment of the work of the Messiah for the people is closely related to the destruction of the rebuilt Temple, which followed about 37 years later. Due to the sufficiency of the atoning sacrifice of the Messiah once for all time, there was no longer a need for sacrifices in the Temple. Then on the Day of Pentecost (which was sometime prior to the Roman army attack on Jerusalem in 70 A. D.), as the priests entered the inter court of the temple, "They felt a quaking, and heard a great noise, and after that they heard a sound as of a great multitude saying, 'Let us remove hence.'"
Josephus, *A History of The Jewish Wars,* Bk. VI, Ch. IV (See page 115)

The presence of the Lord that honored the Levitical sacrifices left the temple and the people of the prince, who will come later, (the antichrist) took advantage and destroyed the city (Jerusalem) and the temple.

→For your people

The prophecy was for Daniel's people, the Hebrews; however, the Gentiles are included as they are also beneficiaries of salvation by grace through faith. The word of the Lord speaking through the written words of the prophet Isaiah saying to the Messiah that the Gentiles are also given to him.

Isaiah 48:6

6 Indeed He says, 'It is too small a thing that You should be My Servant To raise up the tribes of Jacob, And to restore the preserved ones of Israel; I will also give You as a light to the Gentiles, that You should be My salvation to the ends of the earth.'"

1→To finish transgression

A transgression is an act outside of the law. A transgression may be against God or it may be against people.

The Trespass Offering was for "forgiveness for definite acts of sin."[4:3] The trespass offering foreshadowed an aspect of the atoning sacrificial death of the Messiah on the cross. When a trespass offering was given, God looked forward to the atoning sacrificial death of the Messiah on the cross. Since that has been accomplished, there now is no longer a need for the trespass offering, as through faith in the atoning sacrificial death of the Messiah the believer is forgiven.

Isaiah 53:5 Speaks of the fulfillment of the trespass offering by a person.

Isaiah 53:5

5a He was pierced for our transgressions.
The interlinear NIV Heb. Eng. O. T.; John R. Kohlenberger III, (Zondervan)

Isa. 53:8b **For He was cut off from the land of the living; For the transgressions of My people He was stricken.**

Then in Daniel 9: 26b, it is specifically applied to the Messiah, **"Messiah shall be cut off, but not for Himself."**

Then in the New Testament it speaks of the trespass offering being fulfilled by the Messiah, the Lord Jesus.
Colossians 2:13-14
13 And you, being dead in your trespasses and uncircumcision of your flesh, He has made alive together with Him, having forgiven you all trespasses, 14 having wiped out the handwriting of requirements that was against us, which was contrary to us. And He has taken it out of the way, having nailed it to the cross.

It has been finished; it has been accomplished. One only needs to believe on the Lord Jesus and receive what he has already accomplished. When Jesus was upon the cross, He paid the penalty for sin and said, "It is finished."
John 19:30b
30b He said, "It is finished!" And bowing His head, He gave up His spirit.

2→To put an end to sin
The sin offering was for when restitution was not possible. The sin offering provided for one's sinful nature.
Isaiah Chapter 53 speaks of a person being the sin offering.
Isaiah 53:10
10a Yet it pleased the Lord to bruise Him; He has put *Him* to grief. When You make His soul an offering for sin.

Isaiah 53:12
12b Because He poured out his soul unto death, And He was numbered with the transgressors, And He bore the sin of many, And made intercession for the transgressors.
"For in the Sin-offering the blood was poured out at the bottom of the altar."[4:4]

Then the New Testament speaks of the sin offering being fulfilled by the Messiah, the Lord Jesus.
Hebrews 9:26
9:26b He has appeared to put away sin by the sacrifice of Himself.

1 Peter 2:24

24 **Who Himself bore our sins in His own body on the tree, that we having died to sins, might live for righteousness—by whose stripes you were healed.**

2 Corinthians 5:21

21 **For He made Him who knew no sin** *to be* **sin for us, that we might become the righteousness of God in Him.**

3→To make atonement for wickedness, iniquity

The Hebrew word עָוֺן 'āwōn "wickedness, iniquity, often with a focus on the guilt or liability incurred, and the punishment to follow."[4:5] Atonement means covering; it can also mean make reconciliation. and that relates to Leviticus 17:11.

Leviticus 17:11

For the life of the flesh is in the blood, and I have given it to you upon the altar to make atonement for your souls; for it is the blood *that* **makes atonement for the soul.**

Isaiah Chapter 53 speaks of a person making atonement for iniquity.

Isaiah 53:5

5a **But he was pierced for our transgressions, he was crushed for our iniquities.**

The interlinear NIV Heb. Eng. O. T.; John R. Kohlenberger III, (Zondervan)

Isaiah 53:6

6b **We have turned, every one, to his own way; and the Lord has laid on Him the iniquity of us all.**

In the seventy sevens prophecy in Daniel 9:26b it says, **"Messiah shall be cut off, but not for Himself."** The preface in Daniel 9:24 describes the accomplishment of the messiah being cut off. It is **to make atonement for iniquity**, but not for Himself; it is for the people.

Then in the New Testament (speaking of the Lord Jesus), the atoning sacrificial death of the Messiah, Jesus, on the cross paid the penalty for the guilt of wickedness and iniquity for as many as receive him. John 19:34 speaks of the side of Jesus having been pierced while He was on the cross and blood and water came out.

John 19:34
34 But one of the soldiers pierced His side with a spear, and immediately blood and water came out.

Titus 2:14
14 Who gave himself for us, that He might redeem us from all iniquity, and purify unto Himself a peculiar* people, zealous of good works.[4:6] *His own possession

4→To bring in everlasting righteousness

The Burnt Offering represents Justification. However, bulls and goats are not perfect as the Messiah, Jesus is perfect; they cannot pay the penalty for sin nor impute righteousness. The offerings were a foreshadowing of the atoning sacrifice of the Messiah. When offerings were made God looked forward to the atoning sacrificial death of Jesus, the Messiah, on the cross.
Hebrews 10:4
4 For it is not possible that the blood of bulls and goats could take away sins.

Justification is the positive righteousness of Jesus, the Messiah, imputed to the believer. Where in this case, imputed means to be assigned a value beyond what is capable on one's own.
Acts 13:39
39 And by Him everyone who believes is justified from all things from which you could not be justified by the law of Moses.

2 Corinthians 5:21
21 For He made Him who knew no sin to be sin for us, that we might become the righteousness of God in Him.

The atoning sacrificial death of Jesus, the Messiah, on the cross was once for all time.
Hebrews 9:12
12 Not with the blood of goats and calves, but with His own blood He entered the Most Holy Place once for all, having obtained eternal redemption.

5→**To anoint the most holy** *one* 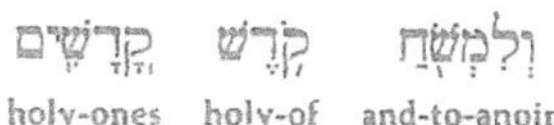

Literally: holy-of holy-ones (some translations add "place," but it is not in the Hebrew text), the Messiah is the Holy-of-Holies personified. Jesus, the Messiah Himself, is the fulfillment of the Holy-of-Holies the Tabernacle represents and the veil in front of the Holy-of-Holies represents his flesh.

God is one God—in three persons—each distinct—yet existing simultaneously.

John 1:1

1 **In the beginning was the Word, and the Word was with God, and the Word was God.**

John 1:14

14 **And the Word became flesh and tabernacled among us.**[4:7]

In the New Testament the Greek word ἐσκήνωσεν is tabernacled

The Word that became flesh is Jesus, the Messiah, the Ruler, who is God incarnate for the purpose of being the atoning sacrifice for our sins because only God is sacrificially holy. He was among us as the fulfilment of the σκηνήν (Greek for tabernacle).

Hebrews 8:5

5 **Who serve the copy and shadow of heavenly things, as Moses was divinely instructed when he was about to make the tabernacle.**[4:8] (the Greek word σκηνήν is translated tabernacle)

Hebrews 10:19-20

19 **Therefore, brethren, having boldness to enter the Holiest by the blood of Jesus, 20 by a new and living way which He consecrated for us, through the veil, that is, His flesh.**

The background to the Messiah as God, born as a child, is found in Isaiah chapter 6. In Isaiah 9:6-7 the Messiah is described as a ruler of which *there will be* no end of His Government. In the seventy sevens prophecy in Daniel 9:25, He is called, **"The Messiah, the Ruler."**

Isaiah 9:6-7a

6 **For unto us a Child is born, unto us a Son is given; and the government will be upon His shoulder. And his name will be called Wonderful, Counselor, Mighty God, Everlasting Father, Prince of Peace. 7 Of the increase of His government and peace** *there will be* **no end.**

The anointing of Jesus by the Holy Spirit was the physical representation of Jesus as the Messiah, the anointed one. The Holy Spirit alighted upon Jesus described as like a dove.
Matthew 3:16-17
16 **When He had been baptized, Jesus came up immediately from the water; and behold, the heavens were opened to Him, and He saw the Spirit of God descending like a dove and alighting upon Him.** 17 **And suddenly a voice** *came* **from heaven, saying, "This is My beloved Son, in whom I am well pleased."**

The Trinity is spoken of in Matthew 3:16-17, the Holy Spirit of God alighting upon Jesus and the Father from heaven saying, **"This is My beloved Son."**

6→To seal up vision and prophecy

Seventy sevens is the timetable to accomplish this prophecy told by Gabriel and many of the visions that Daniel received.
A seal is placed on a document after it is finished. The prophecy will be completed by the end of the seventy sevens.

Modern day theological liberals have been propagating the interpretation that there are three negative phrases and three positive phrases, then applying the negative phrases to the people. However, it has been shown that they are all positive phrases that are aspects of the accomplishments of the Messiah for the people. Furthermore, early Christians interpreted this passage in Daniel that way, as Julius Africanus (160-240 A.D.) wrote:

"For in the Savior's time, or from Him, are transgressions abrogated, and sins brought to an end. And through remission, moreover, are iniquities, along with offences, blotted out by expiation; and an everlasting righteousness is preached, different from that which is by law, and visions and prophecies (are) until John, and the Most Holy is anointed. For before the advent of the Savior these things were not yet, and were therefore only looked for."[4:9]
Julius Africanus *Chronographiai* (XVI)

Chapter 4: Daniel 9:24 the preface to the counting of the seventy sevens that speaks of the work of the Messiah, quotations

4:1. Ada R. Habershon, *The study of the Types* (Grand Rapids: Kregel Pub., 1970) p. 85

4:2. *The Strongest Strong's Exhaustive Concordance of the Bible* (Hebrew word 7620)

4:3. Ada R. Habershon, *The study of the Types* (Grand Rapids: Kregel Pub., 1970) p. 85

4:4. Ibid., p. 93

4:5. *The Strongest Strong's Exhaustive Concordance of the Bible* (Hebrew word 5771)

4:6. *The Interlinear Greek English New Testament,* The Reverend Alfrend Marshall D. Litt. (Samuel Bagster and Sons, London, WI.)

4:7. Ibid.

4:8. Ibid.

4:9. The ANTE-NICENE FATHERS Translations of *The writings of the Fathers down to A.D. 325,* The Rev. Alexander Roberts, D. D. and James Donaldson, LL. D. editors; AMERICAN REPRINT OF THE EDINBURGH EDITION; Volume VI.
(THE CHRISTIAN LITERATURE COMPANY, N. Y., 1890) p. 134
And
(WM. B. EERDMANS PUBLISHING COMPANY Grand Rapids, MI. Photolithoprinted by Cushing – Malloy, Inc. Ann Arbor, MI. 1957) p. 134

Chapter 5
The seventy sevens prophecy told to Daniel by the angel Gabriel after the preface (Daniel 9:25-27)

Daniel 9:25-27
25 **"Know therefore and understand,** *that* **from the going forth of the command to restore and build Jerusalem until Messiah the Prince,** *there shall be* **seven weeks, and sixty-two weeks; The street shall be built again, and the wall, even in troublesome times.**

26 **And after the sixty-two weeks Messiah shall be cut off, but not for Himself; and the people of the prince who** *is* **to come shall destroy the city and the sanctuary. The end of it** *shall be* **with a flood.**
New King James Version (Nashville: Thomas Nelson Inc., 1982)

26c **War will continue until the end, and desolations have been decreed.**
27 **He will confirm a covenant with many for one seven. In the middle of the seven, he will put an end to sacrifice and offering. And on a wing (***of the temple***) he will set up an abomination that causes desolation, until the end that is decreed is poured out on him."**
Interlinear NIV Hebrew-English Old Testament John R. Kohlenberger III (Grand Rapids: Zondervan Publishing House, 1987)

An outline of the order and timing of the Seventy Sevens prophecy after the preface (Daniel 9:25-27)

 ┌ **The issuing of the decree to restore and rebuild Jerusalem**
7x7
It (*Jerusalem*) will be rebuilt with streets and a wall, but in times of trouble.
&
7x62
 └ **until the Messiah, the Ruler, comes there will be**
...seven sevens and sixty-two sevens;

and after the sixty-two sevens, the Messiah will be cut off, but not for Himself.

The people of the ruler who will come will destroy the city and the sanctuary. The end will come like a flood.

War will continue until the end,   and desolations have been decreed.

 ┌ **He will confirm a covenant with many for one seven.**

In the middle of the seven he will put an end to sacrifice and offering.
7x1

On a wing (*of the temple*) he will set up an abomination that causes desolation,
 └ **until the end that is decreed is poured out on him.**

A great number of the events mentioned in the seventy sevens prophecy have already happened and they are widely known historical facts.

The early part of the seventy sevens prophecy has already happened and is historically known; although, certain later parts of the prophecy speak of events that are still in the future. Where an early verse in the prophecy says, **"The people of the prince to come will destroy the city and the sanctuary."** We can say, "The city and the sanctuary were destroyed" because it is a widely known historical fact that the Roman Legions destroyed the city of Jerusalem and the Temple. The popular date for the destruction of Jerusalem by the Roman Legions is in 70 A.D. Julian.

In the seventy sevens prophecy with the coming of the Messiah, the Ruler, a series of interconnected events follow including the destruction of the Jerusalem Temple and beyond that event.

One might ask, "What does the Messiah, who was **cut off** [put to death], **but not for Himself,** have to do with the Jerusalem Temple being destroyed about thirty-seven years later?" The answer is, due to the sufficiency of the work of the Messiah, who was **cut off** [put to death], **but not for Himself,** in order **to atone for wickedness, iniquity,** for those that believe in him; an everlasting atonement was accomplished **to bring in everlasting righteousness** and God began living in those believing in the Messiah. The temple was no longer necessary for sacrifices and God departed from it prior to **the people of the prince to come** destroying it.

Daniel 9:24, the preface to the counting of the seventy sevens is an important introduction that details certain aspects of the accomplishment of the Messiah, who was **cut off** [put to death], **but not for Himself.**

The sacrificial atoning death of Jesus on the cross fulfilled His mission as the **Messiah**. That happened at the time of the first advent, 'appearance,' of the Lord Jesus. In the future at the time of the second advent, 'appearance,' the Lord Jesus will return again as the **Ruler** in great power and glory.

Chapter 6

Considering the edict of Cyrus, the Great, in 538 B.C. as the beginning for the counting of the seven sevens and sixty-two sevens **until the Messiah, the Ruler, comes** as prophesied in Daniel 9:25

There have been several interpreters that have used the date of the edict of Cyrus the Great given in the first year of his reign as the beginning for the counting of seven sevens and sixty-two sevens. The edict of Cyrus I is given in Ezra 1:1-4.

Ezra 1:1-4

1 **Now the first year of Cyrus king of Persia, that the word of the Lord by the mouth of Jeremiah might be fulfilled, the Lord stirred up the spirit of Cyrus king of Persia, so that he made a proclamation throughout all his kingdom, and also** *put it* **in writing saying ,**

2 **Thus says Cyrus king of Persia: All the kingdoms of the earth the Lord God of heaven has given me. And He has commanded me to build Him a house at Jerusalem which** *is* **in Judah. 3 Who** *is* **among you of all his people? May his God be with him, and let him go to Jerusalem which is in Judah, and build the house of the Lord God of Israel (He is God), which** *is* **in Jerusalem. 4 And whoever is left in any place where he dwells, let the men of his place help him with silver and gold, with goods and livestock, besides the freewill offerings for the house of God which** *is* **in Jerusalem.**

The edict of Cyrus the Great to rebuild the Temple was prophesied by Isaiah.

The Lord's intention for the edict of Cyrus is that Jerusalem shall be built and the foundation of the Temple shall be laid.

Isaiah 44:28

28 **Who says of Cyrus, '***He is My*** shepherd*, and he shall perform all My pleasure, saying to Jerusalem, "You shall be built," and to the temple, "Your foundation shall be laid."'**

* literally: **messiah**, 'anointed one,' but not Messiah, the Ruler, as in Daniel. An anointing is for a mission. Cyrus's mission was that the foundation of the Temple shall be laid.

The prophet Haggai marks the end of the desolation of the land that fulfills its seventy years of Sabbath rest.

The prophet Haggai told a priest a riddle to demonstrate that even though they had been permitted to return to build on the city and the Temple they were still unclean. Then after they laid the foundation of the Temple on a day that coincided with the end of the seventy years of desolation of the land, Haggai spoke the word of the Lord blessing them.
(Haggai 2:18 and 19c)

"Consider now from this day forward, from the twenty-fourth day of the ninth month, from the day that the foundation of the LORD'S temple was laid—consider it:…from this day I bless you," (December 18, 520 B.C.).

The edict of Cyrus is not the beginning of the counting of the seventy sevens because the seventy years of Sabbath rest of the land were not over at that time.

The strongest objection to using the edict of Cyrus in 538 B.C. as the beginning of the seventy sevens prophecy is that when Cyrus made his edict, the seventy years of desolation of the land were not completed. The seventy years of rest of the land were not finished until (December 18, 520 B.C.).

Daniel had been reading the prophet Jeremiah and he prayed to the Lord God to tell him what would happen after the seventy years were over. When Cyrus made his edict, the seventy years of desolation were not over, so it does not qualify.

The edict of Cyrus is not the beginning of the counting of the seventy sevens because there was no provision for building materials given at that time.

There is no provision for building materials in the edict of Cyrus for the city of Jerusalem to be built with streets and a wall or a trench (if one accepts that translation). Those that returned to Judah immediately after the edict of Cyrus did not build a wall; hence, they did not accomplish forming a trench along the wall either because news came to Nehemiah that the wall was torn down.

Chapter 7
The decree of Artaxerxes I given to Nehemiah in the month of Nisan (Hebrew) April 3 to May 1, 444 B.C. (Julian), as the beginning of the counting of the seven sevens and sixty-two sevens **until the Messiah, the Ruler, comes** as prophesied in Daniel 9:25

Nehemiah 2:1-9
1 **And it came to pass in the month of Nisan, in the twentieth year of King Artaxerxes, *when* wine *was* before him, that I took the wine and gave it to the king. Now I had never been sad in his presence before.**
2 **Therefore the king said to me, "Why *is* your face sad, since you *are* not sick? This *is* nothing but sorrow of heart." So I became dreadfully afraid,**
3 **and said to the king, "May the king live forever! Why should my face not be sad, when the city, the place of my fathers' tombs, *lies* waste, and its gates are burned with fire?"**
4 **Then the king said to me, "What do you request?" So I prayed to the God of heaven.**
5 **And I said to the king, "If it pleases the king, and if your servant has found favor in your sight, I ask that you send me to Judah, to the city of my fathers' tombs, that I may rebuild it."**
6 **Then the king said to me (the queen also sitting beside him), "How long will your journey be? And when will you return?" So it pleased the king to send me; and I set him a time.**
7 **Furthermore I said to the king, "If it pleases the king, let letters be given to me for the governors *of the region* beyond the River, that they must permit me to pass through till I come to Judah,**
8 **and a letter to Asaph the keeper of the king's forest, that he must give me timber to make beams for the gates of the citadel which *pertains* to the temple, for the city wall, and for the house that I will occupy." And the king granted *them* to me according to the good hand of my God upon me.**
9 **Then I went to the governors *in the region* beyond the River, and gave them the king's letters. Now the king had sent captains of the army and horsemen with me.**

At one time in the Hebrew scriptures, Ezra and Nehemiah were incorporated into one book. There is internal evidence that Nehemiah is the author of Neh. 1:1-7:5, which is a critical passage in order to determine the date of the decree of Artaxerxes I. Evidence for that is that Neh. 1:1 begins, **"The words of Nehemiah the son of Hachaliah**," and throughout the passage Nehemiah refers to himself in the first person as "I."

After the Edit of Cyrus in 538 B.C., some of the Babylonian captives had returned to Judah to build on the city of Jerusalem and the Temple. Nehemiah was among those of the Babylonian captivity that remained and in 444 B.C. he had a position of trust serving the King.

According to the book of Nehemiah chapter one, Nehemiah was at Shushan, 'Susa' in Persia, and he was the king's cupbearer. In the month of Kislev in the twentieth year of the king, Nehemiah received the news that the survivors left from the captivity were in great distress and the walls of Jerusalem were broken down and its gates were burned with fire.

According to 2 Kings 25:8-10, in the nineteenth year of Nebuchadnezzar, king of Babylon (586 B.C.), the captain of the guard of Nebuchadnezzar's army led the destruction of the houses and the Temple in Jerusalem and burned them with fire. The army also broke down the walls of Jerusalem.

2 Kings 25:10

10 And all the army of the Chaldeans who *were with* the captain of the guard broke down the walls of Jerusalem all around.

From 586 B.C., when the walls of Jerusalem were broken down by Nebuchadnezzar's army until, Nehemiah received the news in the month of Kislev in the twentieth year of Artaxerxes I, the walls of Jerusalem had not been repaired for a period of 142 years.

Reviewing then, according to Nehemiah chapter one, in the month of Kislev in the twentieth year of the king, Nehemiah received news that the walls of Jerusalem were still broken down. Then in Chapter two, in the twentieth year of Artaxerxes (the same year of the king as in Chapter one) in the month of Nisan, Nehemiah received letters from Artaxerxes to take to Judah.

Based on the order of the months in the same year of the king, it is evident that Nehemiah is not using the Babylonian way of counting the year of the king because Nisan is the first month and begins the New Year that counted the year of the king on the Babylonian calendar. It is not possible for the month of Kislev to be before the month of Nisan in the same year of the king in the Babylonian way of counting the year of the king. Like the Babylonians, the Hebrews counted Nisan as the first month; however, for civil matters such as counting the New Year that counted the year of the king, the Hebrews from Judah used the month of Tishri, which is the seventh month according to the Hebrew way of counting months. When Tishri is the month that is used to count the number of the year of the king, Kislev is before Nisan in the same year of the king. Therefore, Nehemiah was using Tishri as the first month of the year in counting the year of Artaxerxes I.

In order to determine the year of the king according to the way the Babylonians counted the year of the king, it is necessary to determine the year of the king using Tishri as the first month in counting the year of the king and then use Nisanu as the first month in counting the year of the king. Then the year of the king can be determined according to the Babylonian calendar. The advantage of using the Babylonian calendar is that archaeologists have discovered ancient Babylonian clay tablets that contain astrological information about the moon and the sun during a certain kings' reign that have aided in constructing the Babylonian calendar with Julian calendar dates.

Artakhshasta in the Bible in Ezra and Nehemiah is Artaxerxes I of the Achaemenid dynasty, king of Persia, 464-425 B.C.

On the following page there is a calendar that details the conversion of the twentieth year of Artaxerxes I according to the way Nehemiah counted the year of the king using Tishri as the first month in counting the year of the king to the twenty first year of Artaxerxes I according to the way the Babylonians counted the year of the king using Nisanu as the month that began the New Year.

Julian calendar dates show the date of the first day of the month.

Julian B.C.   Babylonian   Hebrew
Months   Months   Months

(Babylonian New Year, 20th Year Artaxerxes I)
Apr. 13, 445   Nisanu   Nisan
May   Aiaru   Iyyar
Jun.   Simanu   Sivan
Jul.   Duzu   Tammuz
Aug.   Abu   Ab
Sep.   Ululu   Elul
                       (Hebrew New Year, 20th Year of Artaxeres I)
Oct.   Tashritu   Tishri
Nov.   Arahsamnu   Heshvan
Dec   Kislimu   Kislev (News about Jerusalem)
Jan. 4, 444   Tebetu   Tebeth
Feb.   Shabatu   Shebat
Mar.   Addaru   Adar
(Babylonian new year, 21st Year Artaxerxes I)
Apr. 3, 444   Nisanu   Nisan (Decree to rebuild Jerusalem)
May 2, 444   Aiaru   Iyyar

The Babylonian calendar months with Julian calendar dates are based on page 32 in the book *Babylonian Chronology 620 B.C.-A.D.75* by R. A. Parker and W. H. Dubberstein; Wipf & Stock Publishers; Eugene, Oregon; Published 5/1/2007.
Previously published by Brown University Press, 1956.

Nehemiah states that Artaxerxes gave him letters for materials to rebuild Jerusalem in the month of Nisan in the 20th year of Artaxerxes. The diagram shows that the 20th year of Artaxerxes I in the month of Nisan in the way that Nehemiah counted the year of Artaxerxes I beginning with the month of Tishri is the 21st year of Artaxerxes I in the month of Nisanu on the Babylonian calendar. Therefore, the decree to rebuild Jerusalem was made in the month of Nisanu near the beginning of the 21st year of Artaxerxes I on the Babylonian calendar, **April 3 to May 1 of 444 B.C. Julian.**

Since Nehemiah was in Susa when he received the letters from Artaxerxes I, he would have been using Babylonian dates with the exception that he used Tishri as the month that began the New Year; therefore, as was shown on the previous page, Nehemiah received the decree in the month of Nisan, 444 B.C. (April 3 to May 1, 444 B.C. Julian).

The post-exilic calendar used by the Babylonian captives that returned to Judah after the edict of Cyrus in 538 B.C. has been reconstructed for the years from the 14th year of Xerxes, 472 B.C. to the 5th year of Artaxerxes II, 399 B.C., which includes the reigns of Artaxerxes I and Darius II. The reconstruction of the post exilic calendar used in Judah is based on ancient papyrus letters double dated with Jewish and Egyptian solar calendar dates found at Elephantine, Egypt by archaeologists.
See: Siegfried H. Horn and Lynn H. Wood, *The Chronology of Ezra 7, Appendix 3,* Reconstruction of the Jewish calendar at Elephantine (Review and Herald Publishing Association, Washington D. C., 1970)

The post-exilic calendar used Tishri as the first month for counting the year of the king the same way that Nehemiah counted the year of the king while he was in Babylon. If it were the case that Nehemiah used the post-exilic calendar in his writings then Nisan 1 in the 20th year of Artaxerxes I is as follows:

445 B.C. → | 444 B.C. →

Tishri	Mar.	Kis.	Teb.	Sheb.	Adar	**Nisan**	**Lyyar**	Sivan	Tam.	Ab	Elul
10/7	11/6	12/5	1/4	2/2	3/4	**4/2**	**5/2**	5/31	6/30	7/29	8/28

See: Siegfried H. Horn and Lynn H. Wood, *The Chronology of Ezra 7, Appendix 3*, Reconstruction of the Jewish calendar at Elephantine, p. 158 (Review and Herald Publishing Association, Washington D. C., 1970)

The 20th year of Artaxerxes I on the post-exilic calendar used in Judah, Nisan 1 began on April 2, 444 B.C.; whereas in the 21st year of Artaxerxes I on the Babylonian calendar, Nisanu 1 began on April 3, 444 B.C. Both dating systems agreeing within one day with the post-exilic dating being one day earlier.

Seven sevens, rebuilding Jerusalem with streets and a wall in times of trouble as prophesied in Daniel 9:25

As Nehemiah requested, Artaxerxes I gave him letters to present to the governors beyond the river and he was escorted by captains of the army and horsemen.

After the Jews returned from the Babylonian exile there were problems with squatters that had settled on their land.

When Nehemiah came to Jerusalem, he waited three days, all the while not disclosing what God had put in his heart to do at Jerusalem. Then during the night with a few men, he inspected the wall. While riding on an animal, he went out through the valley gate to the Serpent Well and the Refuse Gate, then he went on to the Fountain Gate and to the King's Pool. Around there he came to debris in the way, as he says, **"But *there was* no room for the animal under me to pass,"** (Neh. 2:14b). So, he went up the valley and viewed the wall, (Neh. 2:15). Apparently, he crossed the Kidron Valley and up the Mount of Olives in order to get an overview of the wall; then he returned back to the Valley Gate.

Nehemiah had not yet told the Jews, the priests, the nobles, the officials, or others where he had gone. After he returned, Nehemiah told them, **"Come let us build the wall of Jerusalem, that we may no longer be a reproach,"** (Neh. 2:17b); he told them of the hand of God, which had been good upon him and the words of the king, **so they said, "Let us rise up and build,"** (Neh. 2:18b).

Several groups of Jews worked simultaneously on the wall near their homes. Certain Samaritan officials mocked them at first, then after gaps in the wall began to close, the Samaritan's became threating. After that, those that built on the wall and those that carried burdens did construction work with one hand; and with the other hand carried a weapon, (Neh. 4:17). Whenever they heard the sound of the trumpet, they were to rally there, (Neh. 4:20).

So the wall was finished on the twenty-fifth *day* of Elul, in fifty-two days, (Neh. 6:15).

About six months after Nehemiah received the decree from Artaxerxes I, the wall around the City of David part of Jerusalem, which included the Temple Mount, was finished. The rebuilding of the wall led by Nehemiah did not include Hezekiah's Broad Wall addition to the west of the City of David. After the wall was finished two groups walked around on the wall in different directions and met again.

In order to restore Jerusalem in accordance with the prophecy given to Daniel by the angel Gabriel, the wall needed to be built again around the portion of Jerusalem where the Temple was located. Nehemiah received letters from Artaxerxes I giving him authority to build the wall and he accomplished the building of it.

Nehemiah dealt with many other troubles after the wall was built. Nehemiah returned to Persia in the thirty-second year of Artaxerxes, (Neh. 13:6). At that time Nehemiah had been governor of Judah for twelve years, (Neh. 5:14).

After certain days back in Persia, Nehemiah obtained leave from the king and returned to Jerusalem. Upon returning to Judah, Nehemiah discovered evil things that had been done while he was gone, (Neh. 13:6-7). According to the Hebrew historian, Josephus, Nehemiah lived to an old age.

The decree given to Nehemiah by Artaxerxes I marks the beginning of the counting of the seventy sevens beginning with seven sevens when the streets shall be built again, and the wall, even in troublesome times. The time that Nehemiah was in Jerusalem building the wall and even after that was during the period of the seven sevens.

The following page shows an excavation of Nehemiah's Wall in the Jerusalem City of David excavation showing the first turn in Nehemiah's Wall, which deviated from the previous course of the wall because there was debris in the way. As in Nehemiah 2:14b, Nehemiah said, **"But *there was* no room for the animal under me to pass."**

Nehemiah's Wall in the Jerusalem City of David excavation.
Photographed by the author, Douglas Ophus

Chapter 8

Calculating seven sevens and sixty-two sevens after the decree of Artaxerxes I given to Nehemiah in the month of Nisan (Hebrew) April 3-May 1, 444 B.C. (Julian) **until the Messiah, the Ruler, comes** (as prophesied in Daniel 9:25) using the Julian calendar

From the issuing of the decree until the Messiah, the Ruler, comes there will be seven sevens and sixty-two sevens. In mathematical notation that is (7x7) + (62x7) or (69x7). Based on the 360-day ideal future lunar year that was used in future civil matters in Babylon and certain future Bible prophecies (as explained earlier, see page 20), then (69x7) x 360 days equals 173,880 lunar calendar days. Converting to Julian solar calendar years, 173,880 lunar calendar days divided by 365.25 Julian solar calendar days per year equals 476 Julian solar calendar years.

When we look forward to future dates on the calendar, January dates are closer to our own time than December dates in the same year. When we look backward on the calendar to previous dates, January dates are further away than December dates in the same year.

Method 1: calculating 476 years using the Astronomical system

When calculating a span of years using Julian calendar dates going from B.C. dates to A.D. dates, one needs to be aware that the Julian calendar chronological system does not have a zero; it goes from 1 A.D. to 1 B.C.

Julian calendar chronological system

| 2 B.C. Jan.-Dec. | 1 B.C. Jan.-Dec. | 1 A.D. Jan.-Dec. | 2 A.D. Jan.-Dec. |
| -1 Jan.-Dec. | 0 Jan.-Dec. | +1 Jan.-Dec. | +2 Jan.-Dec. |

Astronomical number system[8:1] (used by astronomers)

| 1 year interval | 1 year interval | 1 year interval |

Since the Julian calendar does not have a zero, a Julian B.C. year number is one number larger than an Astronomical year number. When adding a span of years from B.C. to A.D., the B.C. date needs to be counted one smaller to account for the Julian system not having a zero. An interval of 3 years after Jan. 1, 2 B.C. is (-1 + 3 = 2) or Jan. 1, 2 A.D. Julian, NOT (-2 + 3 = 1) or Jan. 1, 1 A.D. Julian.

Method 1: using the Astronomical number system continued

On the Babylonian calendar Nisanu 1, 444 B.C. began on April 3, 444 B.C. Julian.[8:2] April 3, 444 B.C. Julian converted to Astronomical is April 3, -443 Astronomical, then adding the 476 span of years after April 3, -443 Astronomical years, arrives at April 3, 33 A.D. Julian.

Method 2: calculating a span of 476 years on the Julian calendar

On the Babylonian calendar Nisanu 1, 444 B.C. began on April 3, 444 B.C. Julian,[8:2] then from April 3, 444 B.C. to April 3, 1 B.C. is a span of 443 Julian years. Now, from April 3, 1 B.C. to April 3, 1 A.D. is a span of one year. Therefore, from April 3, 444 B.C. to April 3, 1 A.D. is a span of 444 Julian years. Now, 476 years minis 444 years leaves a remainder of 32 years to be added. Then adding a span of 32 years to April 3, 1 A.D. arrives at April 3, 33 A.D.

A more accurate measure of a span of years would be to convert Julian years to Gregorian years. On the Gregorian calendar leap years divisible by 100 are omitted except for leap years devisable by 400. In 476 Julian years there are 3.76 leap years too many amounting to at least 3.76 days too many. Therefore, April 3, 33 A.D. minis 3.76 days is sometime during March 30, 33 A.D.

Nisan 10, 3793 Hebrew or March 30, 33 A.D. Julian is the day of the triumphal entry of Jesus into Jerusalem.

The decree given to Nehemiah favors an early date in Nisan.

Nehemiah does not say the day in the month of Nisan that he received the decree from Artaxerxes I; however, the decree given to Ezra by Artaxerxes I was on Nisan 1. Ezra traveled from Susa and arrived in Jerusalem on Ab 1. That supports the supposition that Nehemiah also received his decree on Nisan 1, since he also traveled from Susa and arrived in Jerusalem on Ab 1. Some have made the claim that decrees were usually given on the first day of the month.

Ezra 7:8-9

8 And Ezra came to Jerusalem in the fifth month, which *was* the seventh year of the king.

9 On the first *day* of the first month he began *his* journey from Babylon, and on the first *day* of the fifth month he came to Jerusalem, according to the good hand of God upon him.

In the seventh year of Artaxerxes according to Ezra, (which would be the eighth year of Artaxerxes according to the Babylonian way of counting), Ezra left Susa on the first day of the first month (Nisan 1). He came to Jerusalem on the first day of the fifth month (Ab 1). So, it took Ezra and those with him four months to go from Susa to Jerusalem.

If Nehemiah had also left Susa on the first day of the first month (Nisan 1), his journey would have also taken four months because it can be calculated that he also came to Jerusalem on the first day of the fifth month (Ab 1).

The wall was finished in 52 days on the twenty-fifth day of Elul. The month of Elul accounts for 25 of the days building the wall, then there are 52 - 25 = 27 more days to be accounted for. According to the post-exilic calendar on page 158, the first day of Elul in the twentieth year of Artaxerxes I was on 8/28, 444 B.C. Julian, [8:3] then counting backward 27 days, the building of the wall began on 8/1, 444 B.C. Nehemiah waited three days in Jerusalem before he looked at the wall and spoke about rebuilding it. Therefore, 8/1, 444 BC - 3 days is 7/29, 444 B.C., which according to the post exilic calendar on page 158 is Ab 1,[8:4] in the twentieth year of Artaxerxes I, and that is the day that Nehemiah came to Jerusalem, the same day of the same month that Ezra came to Jerusalem.

Chapter 8 Calculating seven sevens and sixty-two sevens after the decree of Artaxerxes I using the Julian calendar, quotations
8:1. Siegfried H. Horn and Lynn H. Wood, *The Chronology of Ezra 7,* (Washington, DC: Review and Herald Publishing Association, 1970) 28
8:2. R. A. Parker and W. H. Dubberstein; *Babylonian Chronology 620 B.C.-A.D.75,* (Eugene, OR: Wipf and Stock Publishers, 2007) p.32 (Previously Published by Brown University Press, 1965)
8:3. Siegfried H. Horn and Lynn H. Wood, *The Chronology of Ezra 7,* p. 158
8:4. Ibid., p.158

Calculating seven sevens and sixty-two sevens after the decree of Artaxerxes I given to Nehemiah in the month of Nisan (Hebrew), Nisanu (Babylonian), in the year of 444 B.C. (Julian) **until the Messiah, the Ruler, comes** (as prophesied in Daniel 9:25) using the Babylonian calendar

Another way of calculating the seven sevens and sixty-two sevens is by using the Babylonian calendar. In mathematical notation that is (7x7) + (62x7) or (69x7). Based on the 360 day. ideal future lunar year that was used in future civil matters in Babylon and certain future Bible prophecies, as explained earlier, then (69x7) x 360 days equals 173,880 lunar calendar days.

The Babylonian calendar is basically a lunar-solar calendar that adds a month every two or three years in order to compensate for seasonal drift; as a result, the length of a calendar year varies. However, every 19 year cycle the seasons on the Babylonian calendar are aligned with the seasons on the solar calendar.

Calculating the number of days in the 19-year cycle is 19 x 365.25 = 6940 days per 19-year cycle. Then 173,880 lunar calendar days divided by 6940 days per 19-year cycle is 25 cycles. Then 25 cycles times 19 years per cycle equals 476 years.

The twentieth year of Artaxerxes I according to Nehemiah's way of counting the year of the king beginning with the month of Tishri compares to the twenty-first year of Artaxerxes I according to the Babylonian way of counting the year of the king beginning with the month of Nisanu; therefore, the decree of Artaxerxes I was given to Nehemiah in the month of Nisanu in the twenty-first year of Artaxerxes I according to the way the Babylonians counted it.

Nisanu is the first month of the year on the Babylonian calendar, so counting 476 years beginning with the month of Nisanu starting with the twenty-first year of Artaxerxes I, arrives at the Nisanu year that fulfills the sixty-nine sevens.

The following page shows Babylonian calendar years with Nisanu as the first month of each year beginning with the twenty-first year of Artaxerxes I with the number of Nisanu months listed, that accounts for a span of 476 Nisanu months. Then the 476th. Nisanu begins the year that completes the 476-year span.

Counting 476 Nisanu months on the Babylonian calendar beginning with the 21st year of Artaxerxes I, which is the 20th year of Artaxerxes I according to Nehemiah

Count number
#　　　　　(Nisanu Babylonian New Year, 21st year Artaxerxes I)
1 444 BC Nisanu Aia Sim Duz Abu Ulu Tas Ara Kis Teb Sha Add A II
　　　4/3　　　　　　　　　　　　　　　　↑ 443 B.C.
#　　　　　(Nisanu Babylonian New Year, 22nd. year Artaxerxes I)
2 443 BC Nisanu Aia Sim Duz Abu Ulu Tas Ara Kis Teb Sha Add
　　　4/22　　　　　　　　　　　　　　　↑ 442 BC

Etc., etc.

#　　　　　(Nisanu Babylonian New Year, Year 311 Seleucid era)
444 1 BC Nisanu Aia Sim Duz Abu Ulu Tas Ara Kis Teb Sha Add A II
　　　3/26　　　　　　　　　　　　　　　↑ 1 A.D.
#　　　　　(Nisanu Babylonian New Year, Year 312 Seleucid era)
445 1 AD Nisanu Aia Sim Duz Abu Ulu Tas Ara Kis Teb Sha Add
　　　4/14　　　　　　　　　　　　　　　↑ 2 A.D.

Etc., etc.

#　　　　　(Nisanu Babylonian New Year, Year 342 Seleucid era)
475 31 AD Nis Aia Sim Duz Abu Ulu Tas Ara Kis Teb Sha Add
　　　4/12　　　　　　　　　　　↑ 32 A.D.
#　　　　　(Nisanu Babylonian New Year, Year 343 Seleucid era)
476 32 AD Nis Aia Sim Duz Abu Ulu Tas Ara Kis Teb Sha Add A II
　　　4/1　　　　　　　↑　　　　　　　↑ 1/21 2/20 3/21
　　　　　　　　　　　↑　　　　　　　↑ 33 A.D.
　　　Jewish calendar　　↑ Tis Mar Kis Teb She Ada **Nis**
　　　　　　　　　　　↑ (Heb. N.Y. 3793) 1/21 2/20 **3/21**

The Babylonian calendar months with Julian calendar dates are based on pages 32, 45 and 46 in the book *Babylonian Chronology 620 B,C.-A.D.75* by R. A. Parker and W. H. Dubberstein; Wipf & Stock Publishers; Eugene, Oregon; Published 5/1/2007. Previously published by Brown University Press, 1956.

In the Julian calendar year of 33 A.D., the Babylonian calendar has both Addaru and Addaru II; however, the Hebrew calendar in 33 A.D. has Adar, but not the intercalary month Adar I that would be followed by Adar II. As a result, the Babylonian month Addaru II, that is the last month of the year on the Babylonian calendar begins on March 21, 33 A.D. and the Hebrew month Nisan that is counted as the first month on the Hebrew calendar, also begins on March 21, 33 A.D. Therefore, Nisan 10, the day of the triumphal entry of Jesus, would be March 30, 33 A.D. and Nisan 14, the day of the crucifixion of Jesus, would be April 3, 33 A.D.

Therefore, counting 476 'Nisanu years' after the 21st year of Artaxerxes I, (which is the 20th. Year of Artaxerxes I according to Nehemiah), is the Hebrew month of Nisan that is in the year 33 A.D. on the Julian calendar. The month of Nisan in 33 A.D. is the month of the triumphal entry, the crucifixion, and the resurrection of Jesus.

In order to count 476 'Nisanu years' after the 21st. Year of Artaxerxes I on the Babylonian calendar, (which is the 20th. Year of Artaxerxes I according to Nehemiah), it is not necessary to use the Julian calendar. It may be calculated using only the Babylonian calendar. It is not necessary to use the Julian calendar in terms of the year, the month, the day, and the change from B.C. years to A.D. years. An ancient person could have made a prediction of the coming of the Messiah using the lunar calendar. As far as the calculation using the Babylonian calendar is concerned, dates on the Julian calendar serve as a reference in order to help modern persons conceptualize it.

Counting 476 'Nisanu years' beginning with the twenty-first year of Artaxerxes I on the Babylonian calendar is the month Nisan on the Hebrew calendar in 33 A.D. on the Julian calendar. The Hebrew month of Nisan in 33 A.D. Julian is the month of the triumphal entry, crucifixion, and resurrection of Jesus.

Chapter 10
Dating the year of the crucifixion of Jesus using the Gospels

The day of the week Jesus was crucified was a day before the Sabbath, the sixth day of the week, a Friday.
John 19:31
31 **Therefore, because it was the Preparation *Day,* that the bodies should not remain on the cross on the Sabbath (for that Sabbath was a high day).**

Jesus was crucified on the Day of Preparation, the day before the Passover when the lambs were sacrificed for the Passover that began after sunset, which counted as the next day according to the Jews. The Sabbath that year was a high Sabbath because the Passover that year was on the Sabbath, the seventh day of the week. Therefore, Jesus was crucified on the day before the seventh day, the sixth day of the week, the day we call Friday.

The Passover is celebrated on Nissan 15. Jesus was crucified on the Day of Preparation, a day before the Passover; therefore, Jesus was crucified on Nissan 14, which was a Friday that year.

John The Baptist began baptizing in the fifteenth year of Tiberius

An early Christian anchor date in the Bible is when John the Baptist began baptizing in the wilderness. Luke 3:1-3 speaks of John son of Zacharias [John the Baptist], preaching a baptism of repentance in the fifteenth year of the reign of Tiberius Caesar.

The fifteenth year of Tiberius equates to 29 A.D. Julian

Augustus died in August of 767 A.U.C. 'Ab Urbe Condita' (From the Founding of the City, i.e. Rome). Tiberius was appointed emperor by the Roman Senate in September. Using the ascension method of dating, Tiberius' first year began in 768 A.U.C.

In the Julian calendar as the Christian era calendar proposed by Dionysius Exiguus, the year 1 Anni Domini Jesu Christi (years of our Lord Jesus Christ) equates to 754 Ab Urbe Condita, then the 1st year of Tiberius 768 A.U.C. minus 754 equates to 14 A.D. and his 15th year was 14 A.D. plus 15 years which equals 29 A.D. Therefore, John began baptizing in 29 A.D. Julian.

John the Baptist began baptizing in the summer of 29 A.D. John prepared the way for Jesus with his baptism of repentance. Luke mentions many groups of people that came to be baptized by John, then he says, **"when all the people were baptized…Jesus was also baptized**," (Luke 3:21). When Jesus was baptized, it came to pass the Holy Spirit alighted upon Jesus for the purpose of impowering him in his messianic mission. Then the Spirit led Jesus into the wilderness for 40 days and during that time he was tempted by the devil. Following that Luke speaks of Jesus going to Galilee and speaking in the synagogues and healing people before Jesus called four fishermen as disciples. So, a substantial amount of time had elapsed since John the Baptist begin baptizing until Jesus called Simon Peter, his brother Andrew and (James and John the sons of Zebedee). A sufficient amount of time that they were apparently not called by Jesus to be disciples until after the Passover in the spring of 30 A.D. for the following reasons.

The Gospel of John speaks of three Passovers after John the Baptist speaks of baptizing Jesus in John 1:29-34. The first Passover spoken of after Jesus was baptized is in John 2:13, the second is John 6:4, and the third is John 11: 55. The Passover the day after Jesus was crucified on Nissan 14, a Friday that year.

The Julian calendar, the Jewish calendar, and the Gregorian calendar all agree on the day of the week, (even though the Gregorian calendar advanced ten days in order to correct for the equinox when October 4, 1582 was followed by October 15, 1582; the days of the week did not change with the change of the date).

John mentions three Passovers after Jesus was baptized in 29 A.D.; however, Nissan 14 was not on a Friday in 32 A.D., but Nissan 14 was on a Friday in 33 A.D. Therefore, The Passover after the crucifixion of Jesus in John 11:55 was in 33 A.D. (which has been verified astronomically). The Passover in John 6:4 was in 32 A.D. The Passover in John 2:13 was in 31 A.D. and the Passover in 30 A.D. was apparently before John became a disciple of Jesus.

Jewish Calendar
Nisan 9-22, 3793

1st Day	2nd Day	3rd Day	4th Day	5th Day	6th Day	Sabbath
Sunday	Monday	Tuesday	Wednesday	Thursday	Friday	Saturday
9	**10** Lamb Triumphal Entry of Jesus	11	12	13	**14** Day of Preparation Crucifixion of Christ Red Moon	**15** Passover
16 Firstfruits Resurrection of Jesus	17	18	19	20	21	22

Julian Calendar
March 29-April 11, 33 A.D.

Sunday	Monday	Tuesday	Wednesday	Thursday	Friday	Saturday
29	**30** Lamb Triumphal Entry of Jesus	31	1	2	**3** Day of Preparation Crucifixion of Christ Red Moon	**4** Passover
5 Firstfruits Resurrection of Jesus	6	7	8	9	10	11

An outline of the order and timing of the seventy sevens prophecy told to Daniel by the angel Gabriel

⌐ **The issuing of the decree to restore and rebuild Jerusalem.**
7x7
It (*Jerusalem*) will be rebuilt with streets and a trench, but in times of trouble.
&
7x62
∟ **until the Messiah, the ruler, comes there will be**
…seven sevens and sixty-two sevens.

After the sixty-two sevens, the Messiah will be cut off, but not for Himself

The people of the ruler who will come will destroy the city and the sanctuary. The end will come like a flood.

War will continue until the end,   and desolations have been decreed.

⌐ **He will confirm a covenant with many for one seven.**

In the middle of the seven he will put an end to sacrifice and offering.
7x1

On a wing (*of the temple*) he will set up an abomination that causes desolation,
∟ **until the end that is decreed is poured out on him.**

The decree of Artaxerxes
in the month of Nisan on
the Hebrew calendar
(April 3-May 1, 444 B.C.
Julian) to Nehemiah that
marks the beginning of
the counting of the seven
sevens and sixty-two
sevens

The triumphal entry of
Jesus as the Messiah on
Nisan 10, 3793 Hebrew
March 30, 33 A.D. Julian

Jesus died on the cross
Nisan 14, 3793 Hebrew
April 3, 33 A.D. Julian.
Messiah shall be cut off,
but not for Himself

The Romans destroyed
the city of Jerusalem
and the temple in 70 A.D.
That was followed by the
desolation of Judea in
135 A.D.

On May 14, 1948 A.D.
the declaration of the
new State of Israel to
begin May 15, 1948 A.D.
marks the end of the
desolations

The United Nations
 may be where
 the treaty with many
participants
 might be ratified

The triumphal entry of Jesus into Jerusalem through the Eastern Gate on Nisan 10 (Hebrew) March 30, 33 A.D. (Julian) that fulfills **until the Messiah, the Ruler comes** as prophesied in Daniel 9:25

Nisan 10 was the day lambs to be sacrificed for the Passover were presented to the priests to be inspected for blemishes. On the day of the triumphal entry of Jesus into Jerusalem, He presented Himself to the priests and the people as the perfect Lamb of God.

The time for when the Messiah will come is given in chapters 8 and 9. From the issuing of the decree there will be seven sevens and sixty-two sevens which leads immediately to the Hebrew month of Nisan in 33 A.D. Julian, the month of the triumphal entry, the crucifixion, and the resurrection of Jesus.

As Jesus made his journey from Galilee to Jerusalem, at a certain village he told ten lepers to show themselves to the priests and as they went, they were cleansed of their leprosy.

As they were going up to Jerusalem, Jesus took the disciples aside and prophesied his death and resurrection for the third time, as he had told them two times earlier.

Luke 18:31-34; also, Matt. 20:17-19, and Mark 10:32-34

31 Then He took the twelve aside and said to them, "Behold, we are going up to Jerusalem, and all things that are written by the prophets concerning the Son of Man will be accomplished. 32 For He will be delivered to the Gentiles and will be mocked and insulted and spit upon. 33 They will scourge *Him* and kill him. And the third day He will rise again."

34 But they understood none of these things; this saying was hidden from them, and they did not know the things which were spoken.

Later as He was coming near Jericho, Jesus healed two blind men along the road who called out to Him. As Jesus journeyed toward the Mount of Olives a multitude of people were following him because of the miracle healings they had seen. When Jesus and his disciples came near to the Mount of Olives, He sent two of his disciples into the village to bring a donkey colt to Him upon which no one had ever sat.

Luke 19:29-35 and 36-38

29 And it came to pass, when He drew near to Bethphage and Bethany, at the mountain called Olivet, *that*
He sent two of his disciples, 30 saying, "Go into the village opposite *you,* **where as you enter you will find a colt tied, on which no one has ever sat. Loose it and bring** *it here.* **31 And if anyone asks you, 'Why are you loosing** *it*?' **Thus you shall say to him, 'Because the Lord has need of it.'" 32 So those who were sent went their way and found** *it* **just as He had said to them. 33 But as they were loosing the colt, the owners of it said to them, 'Why are you loosing the colt?" 34 And they said, "The Lord has need of him."**
35 Then they brought him to Jesus. And they threw their own clothes on the colt, and they set Jesus on him.

As Jesus rode the donkey, people laid their garments on the road even before the descent down the Mount of Olives. As they neared the descent of the Mount of Olives the multitude began shouting and praising God for the mighty works they had seen.
36 And as he went *many* **spread their clothes on the road.**
37 Then, as He was now drawing near the descent of the Mount of Olives, the whole multitude of the disciples began to rejoice and praise God with a loud voice for all the mighty works they had seen, 38 saying: "'Blessed is the King who comes in the name of the Lord!" Peace in Heaven and glory in the highest!"

Along the way they came to the causeway and the stairway that led to the eastern gate. Matthew 21:5 quotes Zechariah 9:9 as a fulfilment of Jesus bringing salvation, riding a donkey.
Zechariah 9:9
9 Rejoice greatly, O daughter of Zion! Shout, O daughter of Jerusalem! Behold, your king is coming to you; He *is* **just and having salvation, Lowly and riding on a donkey, a colt, the foal of a donkey.**

However, the fulfillment of Zechariah 9:9 does not require that Jesus rode the donkey through the Eastern Gate, although, He may have or He may have first dismounted and walked through the gate. The exact placement of the causeway has not been determined yet because most of it above ground was destroyed by the Romans.

When those in Jerusalem heard that Jesus was coming, many carrying palm branches went out to meet him. As Jesus entered through the Eastern Gate into the Temple area, his disciples were quoting from Psalm 118:26a, **"Blessed *is* he who comes in the name of the Lord!"**

The Pharisees were upset because the crowd was saying that Jesus was coming in the name of the Lord.

39 And some of the Pharisees called to Him from the crowd, "Teacher, rebuke your disciples." 40 But He answered and said to them, "I tell you that if these should keep silent, the stones would immediately cry out," (Luke 19:39-40).

The tenth day of the month of Nisan is the day that a lamb without blemish was chosen for the Passover and presented to the priests. Jesus as the Lamb of God having salvation for the sins of believers, entered Jerusalem through the Eastern Gate on the tenth day of Nisan. After Jesus entered through the Eastern Gate and presented himself to the people, he cleansed the Temple. Then the blind and the lame came to Jesus and He healed them. As the hour was already late, Jesus then went to Bethany with the twelve.

When Jesus returned to Jerusalem, He answered the chief priests, the scribes, and the elders who questioned His authority. He also answered the Pharisees question about paying taxes, the Sadducees question about the Resurrection, and He told the people many parables.

As the time to eat the Passover was approaching, Jesus sent Peter and John instructing them that as they entered the city, they would meet a man carrying a pitcher of water, and should follow him to the house he entered. They spoke to the master of the house as Jesus had instructed them and he showed them an upper room where they made ready for the Passover. After supper, Jesus instituted the celebration of the remembrance of Him.

Luke 22:19-20

19 "And He took bread, gave thanks and broke *it,* and gave it to them, saying, "This is My body which is given for you; do this in remembrance of Me." 20 Likewise He also took the cup after supper, saying, "This cup is the new covenant in My blood, which is shed for you."

After that Jesus went to the Mount of Olives to pray, and his disciples went with Him. As Jesus was in prayer, while knowing the burden of sin he was about to bear, He was in such travail that He sweat great drops of blood on the ground.

Luke 22:44

44 And being in agony, He prayed more earnestly. Then His sweat became like great drops of blood falling down to the ground.

The sacrifice of the Red Heifer is a representation of an aspect of the atoning sacrificial death of Jesus on the cross. An early rabbinical writing explains the sacrifice of the red heifer.

Middoth 1 Mishnah 3: and the Eastern Gate over which was portrayed the palace of Shushan [Susa] and through which the High Priest who burnt the Red Heifer and all who assisted with it used to go forth to the Mount of Olives.

The Red Heifer was brought across a causeway toward the Mount of Olives.

Parah 3 Mishnah 6: a causeway was made from the temple mount to the Mount of Olives, being constructed of arches above arches, each arch placed directly above each pier [of the arch below] as a protection against a grave in the depths, whereby the priest who was to burn the cow, the cow itself and all who aided in its preparation went forth to the Mount of Olives.

Once the Red Heifer was on the Mount of Olives, it was sacrificed at a place in line with the entrance of the temple. From the Mount of Olives, the priest would look over the eastern wall into the entrance of the temple. In order to do that the priest might have also needed to look through the Nicanor Gate, which was in front of the temple.

Middoth 2 Mishnah 4: All the walls there were high, save only the eastern wall, so that the priest that burn the Red Heifer might while standing on the top of the Mount of Olives by directing his gaze carefully see the door of the Hekal [Temple] at the time of the sprinkling of the blood.

The priest sprinkled the blood of the Red Heifer seven times from the Mount of Olives toward the Holy of Holies in the temple and the blood touched the ground in the direction of the Garden of

Gethsemane, which was between the Mount of Olives and the Temple Mount.

Mishnah Parah 3.9: seven times he dipped his finger in the blood and sprinkled it towards the Holy of Holies dipping once again for each sprinkling

Mishnah Parah 4.2: If the blood was sprinkled but not exactly in the direction of the entrance of the Holy of Holies it is invalid.

The popular belief that all paths lead to the same place is false. Jesus said, **"straight *is* the gate, and narrow *is* the way, which leadeth onto life, and few there are that find it,"** (Matthew 7:14). *The Interlinear Greek- English New Testament,* The Reverend Alferd Marshall (London: Samuel Bagster and Sons Limited, 1958)

The Temple on the Temple Mount in the Israeli Museum model of Jerusalem before 70 A.D.

After Jesus had prayed that same night, a detachment with officers from the chief priests and Pharisees came led by Judas for he knew where Jesus often prayed, and he had been paid thirty pieces of silver to betray him. Then Judas greeted Jesus as rabbi and kissed him as a sign. As they came to lay hands on Jesus, one of those with him swung a sword and cut off the right ear of a servant of the high priest. **But Jesus answered and said, "Permit even this." And He touched his ear and healed him,** (Luke 22:51). Jesus requested him to put his sword in its place and He said, **"Or do you not think that I cannot now pray to My Father, and He will provide Me with more than twelve legions of angels?" "How then could the Scriptures be fulfilled, that it must happen thus?"** (Matthew 26:53-54). After Jesus spoke to the multitude that came with swords and clubs the disciples fled.

The officers arrested Jesus, **"And they led Him away to Annas first, for he was the father-in-law of Caiaphas who was high priest that year,** (John 18:13). Peter and another disciple (probably John) followed them. Now that disciple that was known to the high priest (probably Annas, who was high priest from 7 A.D. to 14 A.D. when he was deposed by the Romans) went into the courtyard of the high priest where they had brought Jesus. **Then the servant girl who kept the door said to Peter, "You are not also *one* of this Man's disciples, are you?" He said, "I am not,"** (John 18:17). The high priest (Annas) questioned Jesus about his doctrines and Jesus replied that He had spoken openly to the world in the Synagogues and the Temple. **Then Annas sent him bound to Caiaphas the high priest,** (John 18:24).

As Peter warmed himself by the fire, he was accused of being a disciple and he denied it. Then a relative of him whose ear Peter had cut off, spoke of seeing him in the garden. **Peter then denied again; and immediately a rooster crowed,** (John 18:27). And then Peter remembered Jesus saying to him, **"Before the rooster crows you will deny Me three times,"** (Matthew 26:75b). Peter went out and wept because he had boasted earlier that he would not betray Jesus. In that way Peter was humbled.

At the Palace of the high priest (Caiaphas was the high priest at that time) the council of the Sanhedrin questioned Jesus, 67 **"If you are the Christ, tell us." But He said to them, "If I tell you,**

you will by no means believe. 68 And if I also ask *you*, you will by no means answer Me or let *Me* go. 69 Hereafter the Son of Man will sit on the right hand of the power of God." 70 Then they all said, "Are you then the Son of God?" So He said to them, "You rightly say that I am." 71 And they said, "What further testimony do we need? For we have heard it ourselves from His own mouth," (Luke 22:67-71).

Then early in the morning, the Sanhedrin took Jesus before Pontius Pilate, the Roman Prefect, at the Praetorium. **But they themselves did not go into the Praetorium lest they should be defiled, but that they might eat the Passover,** (John 18:28b). So Pilate came out to them and they accused Jesus of **saying that He Himself is Christ, a king. 3 Then Pilate asked Him, saying, "Are You the King of the Jews?" He answered, him and said, "It is as you say." 4 So Pilate said to the chief priests and the crowd, "I find no fault in this man,** (Luke 23:2d-4).

27 And while He was being accused by the chief priests and elders, He answered nothing. 13 Then Pilate said to him, "Do You not hear how many things they testify against You?" 14 But He answered him not one word, so that the governor marveled greatly,** (Matthew 27:12-14). 5 **But they were the more fierce, saying, "He stirs up the people, teaching throughout all Judea, beginning from Galilee to this place." 6 When Pilate heard of Galilee, he asked if the Man were a Galilean. 7 And as soon as he knew that He belonged to Herod's jurisdiction, he sent Him to Herod, who was also in Jerusalem at the time,** (Luke 23:5-7).

Herod Antipas was glad to see Jesus because he had heard of Jesus and hoped to see a miracle done by Him. Herod Antipas questioned Jesus and the chief priests and scribes stood accusing Him, but Jesus did not answer them. Then Herod and his men put a robe on Jesus, mocked Him, and sent Him back to Pilate.

Fulfilling Isaiah 53:7 and many other passages in Isaiah
Isaiah 53:7
7 He was oppressed and He was afflicted, yet He opened not His mouth; He was led as a lamb to the slaughter, and as a sheep before its shearers is silent, so he opened not His mouth.

Then Pilate 14 **Said to them, "You have brought this Man to me, as one who misleads the people. And indeed, having examined** *Him* **in your presence, I have found no fault in this Man concerning those things of which you accuse Him; 15 no, neither did Herod, for I sent you back to him; and indeed nothing deserving death has been done by Him,"** (Luke 23:14-15).

39 **"But you have a custom that I should release someone to you at the Passover. Do you therefore want me to release to you the King of the Jews?" 40 Then they all cried again saying, "Not this Man, but Barabbas!" Now Barabbas was a robber.** (John 18:39-40). 22 **Pilate said to them, "What then shall I do with Jesus who is called Christ?"** *They* **all said to him, "Let Him be crucified!"** (Matthew 27:22). 26 **Then he released Barabbas to them; and when he had scourged Jesus, he delivered** *Him* **to be crucified,** (Matthew 27:26). Then the solders took Jesus into the Praetorium, put a crown of thorns on His head, a robe on him and spat on him. 31 **And when they had mocked Him, they took the robe off Him, put His** *own* **clothes on Him, and led Him away to be crucified,** (Matthew 27:31).

22. **And they brought Him to the place Golgotha, which is translated, place of a scull,** (Mark 15:22).

On the Day of Atonement, which was for all the people, Aaron, the high priest, was to cast lots between two goats. 8 **Then Aaron shall cast lots for the two goats: one lot for the Lord and the other lot for the scapegoat. 9 And Aaron shall bring the goat on which the Lord's lot fell, and offer it as a sin offering. 10 But the goat on which the lot fell to be the scapegoat shall be presented alive before the Lord, to make atonement upon it,** *and* **to let it go as the scapegoat into the wilderness,** (Leviticus 16:8-10).

In Lev. 16:20-22 Arron laid his hands on the head of the scapegoat (goat of removal) and confessed the sins of the people, then it was led away from the presents of the people representing the removal of their sins. So likewise, the Lord's goat and the scapegoat both represent the Messiah, Jesus, in that Jesus was led out to the place called Golgotha and there He was crucified as a sin offering.

Israeli Museum model of the city of Jerusalem before 70 A.D.

Chapter 12

The Crucifixion of Jesus, the Messiah, our Paschal Lamb, on the Day of Preparation when the Passover Lamb is sacrificed that fulfills **Messiah shall be cut off, but not for Himself** as prophesied in Daniel 9:26

Artwork depicting the darkness that occurred for three hours during the day while the Messiah, the Ruler, Jesus was on the cross.

John 1:29
29 **The next day John* saw Jesus coming toward him, and said, "Behold! The Lamb of God who takes away the sin of the world!"** *John the Baptist

Justin Martyr (100-165 A.D.) wrote an early Christian description of a cross by comparing it to a human with arms starched out.

"And the human form differs from that of the irrational animals in nothing else than in its being erect and having the hands stretched out, and having on the face extended from the forehead what is called the nose, through which there is breath for the living creature—and this shows no other form than that of the cross. And so it was said through the prophet, 'The breath before our face is Christ the Lord.[12:1]'"
Justin Martyr, 1st *Apology,* 55 (151-155 A.D.)
12:1 St. Justin Martyr, The First and Second Apologies, trans. Leslie William Barnard (N.Y., Mahwah, NJ: Paulist Press, 1997) p. 62-63

And after the sixty-two sevens the Messiah shall be cut off, but not for Himself (Daniel 9:26)

Pilate had Jesus scourged with a whip thinking that it would satisfy the angry crowd. The Roman solders put a purple robe on Jesus and a crown of thorns on his head. **Then they said, "Hail, King of the Jews!" And they struck Him with their hands,** (John 19:3). They meant it in jest; however, in point of fact, He is the Messiah, then and now, the Ruler of the Jews and all creation.

After the chief priests and officers kept calling for him to be crucified, Pilate relented and delivered Him to be crucified. Then, Jesus went out to Golgotha and there they crucified Him.
John 19:17-19
17 **And He bearing His cross, went out to a place called** *the place of* **a skull which is called in the Hebrew, Golgotha**, 18 **where they crucified Him, and two others with Him, one on either side, and Jesus in the center.** 19 **Now Pilate wrote a title and put** *it* **on the cross. And the writing was: JESUS OF NAZARETH, THE KING OF THE JEWS.**

The title that was placed on the cross that Jesus was crucified on was written in Hebrew, Greek, and Latin. It was another case of ironic truth, and since it was near the city it upset the chief priests, who wanted it changed to **He said, "I am the king of the Jews,"** (John 19:21b). **Pilate answered, "What I have written, I have written,"** (Luke 19:22). Jesus was crucified the third hour of the day after dawn. **Now it was the third hour, and they crucified Him,** (Mark 15:25).

Then after Jesus had been on the cross for three hours, it became dark as night from the sixth hour until the ninth hour and during that time there was an earthquake.
Matthew 27:45-46
45 **Now from the sixth hour until the ninth hour there was darkness over all the land.** 46 **And about the ninth hour Jesus cried out with a loud voice, saying,** *"Eli, Eli, lama sabachthani?"* **that is,** *My God, My God, why have You forsaken Me?"*

The atoning death of the Messiah, Jesus, was sacrificial in that by His own will, He paid the penalty for our sins.
Luke 23:46
46 **And when Jesus had cried out with a loud voice, He said, "Father, 'into Your hands I commit My spirit.'" Having said this, He breathed His last.**

After the ninth hour it became light again until sunset, and since after sunset the Sabbath would begin, the Jews asked that the legs of the crucified ones should be broken that they might die quicker.
John 19:31
31 **Therefore, because it was the Preparation *Day*, that the bodies should not remain on the cross on the Sabbath (for that Sabbath was a high day), the Jews asked Pilate that their legs might be broken, and *that* they might be taken away.**

John 19: 33-34
33 **But when they came to Jesus and saw that He was already dead, they did not break His legs 34 But one of the soldiers pierced His side with a spear, and immediately blood and water came out.**

John 19:36
36 **For these things were done that the scriptures should be fulfilled, *"Not one of His bones shall be broken."***
A sacrificial lamb was to be without blemish, without any broken bones.
Joseph of Arimathea, who was a disciple of Jesus, but secretly, received permission from Pilate to take away the body of Jesus, (John 19:38).

John 19:40-42
40 **Then they took the body of Jesus, and bound it in strips of linen with the spices, as the custom of the Jews is to bury.**
41 **Now in the place where He was crucified there was a garden, and in the garden a new tomb in which no one had yet been laid. 42 So there they laid Jesus, because of the Jews' Preparation *Day*, for the tomb was nearby.**

Mark 15:25 says, "**Now it was the third hour, and they crucified Him,**" and Matthew 27:45 says, "**Now from the sixth hour until the ninth hour there was darkness over all the land.**"

In these verses it is obvious that they are speaking of hours from sunrise to sunrise rather than from sunset to sunset. Since sunrise in Israel during the time of the Passover is about 6:00 A.M., the third hour would be 9:00 A.M., and darkness from the sixth hour until the ninth hour would be from 12:00 P.M., noon, until 3:00 P.M.

The synoptic gospels, Matthew, Mark, and Luke, speak of Jesus and the disciples eating the Passover. Then at a later time in the Gospel of John when Jesus was brought before Pilate by the Sanhedrin, the Sanhedrin did not want to enter the Praetorium because they had not eaten the Passover yet. One plausible explanation for Jesus and the disciples eating the Passover before the Sanhedrin is that the Galileans counted days from sunrise to sunrise whereas the Sanhedrin counted from sunset to sunset. In that way Jesus ate the Passover counting days from sunrise to sunrise and was crucified at the time lambs were being sacrificed in the Temple counting days from sunset to sunset. In that way the evening after sunset when Jesus and the disciples ate the Passover was the beginning of the day that the Sanhedrin sacrificed the lambs in the Temple and Jesus was crucified that day at 9:00 A.M.

Messiah shall be cut off (Daniel 9:26)

The Hebrew word מָשִׁיחַ 'Masiah' that occurs in the Old Testament is translated Χριστός 'Christos' in the New Testament that is written mostly in the Greek language, it means 'Anointed *One*.'

John 1:41
41 **He first found his own brother Simon, and said to him, "We have found the Messiah" (which is translated, the Christ).**

Messiah means 'Anointed *One*,' an anointing is the presence of God for a mission. The mission of the Messiah in Daniel 9:26 is to be **cut off, but not for Himself.** Isaiah 53:1-12 is an amazing passage that prophesies about Jesus. The prophecies in Isaiah were written before the prophecies in Daniel, so the term cut off in Daniel can be understood in light of Isaiah chapter 53. Isaiah 53:8 is pertinent to the Messiah being cut off, but not for Himself.

Isaiah 53:8
8b For He was <u>cut off</u> from the land of the living; For the transgressions of my people He was stricken.

He was <u>cut off</u> from the land of the living implies a violent action taken against Him that caused His death, **but not for Himself**; His death was an atoning sacrificial death in that by His death, **He bore the sin of many**, (Isaiah 53:12b).

The day of the crucifixion of Jesus was on the Day of preparation for the Passover that was also the day before the Sabbath that year

John 19:31 informs us that Jesus was crucified on the Day of Preparation. The Day of Preparation is the day when the lamb without blemish was sacrificed for the Passover. Exodus 12:1-28 describes the first Passover when the children of Israel were captives in Egypt. A male lamb without blemish was to be chosen on the tenth day and sacrificed on the fourteenth day of the first month. They were to take some of the blood of the lamb and put it on the two door posts and the lintel over the doorway of the house where they ate the lamb. The lamb was to be roasted with fire and eaten that night, which according to the Jewish way of counting days is the next day, and it is to be called the Lord's Passover. The Lord said, **"When I see the blood I will Passover you,"** (Ex. 12:13). In that way no one in that house would be under the plague of death.

John 19:31 also informs us that on the day when Jesus was crucified the next day was a Sabbath that was a high day. Therefore, Jesus was crucified on the sixth day, a Friday, and the next day was a Sabbath that was a high day because it was also the Day of the Passover. The first month is the month of Nisan. The Day of Preparation is the fourteenth day of the first month. Then the day when Jesus was crucified was Nisan 14 which was a Friday that year and the Passover on Nisan 15 was a Sabbath that year.

Jesus was crucified at the third hour. The third hour is one-half way between sunrise and noon, about 9:00 A.M. in the forenoon. While Jesus was on the cross, it was dark from the sixth hour until the ninth hour, which is from noon until one-half way between noon and sunset, about 3:00 P.M. in the afternoon. Then about the ninth hour, which is 3:00 P.M., Jesus said, **"My God, My God, why have You forsaken Me?"** (Matt. 27:46b)

When Jesus spoke of God forsaking Him, he was not only quoting a prophetic passage in Psalm 22:1, He was speaking of an actual true event. The darkness from the sixth hour until the ninth hour represents a time when God, the Father, could not bear to look upon the Son, the Lord Jesus, the Messiah, during the time He was bearing the sins of the world.

When Jesus was on the cross, it was dark from the sixth hour (noon) until the ninth hour (3:00 P.M.). It was dark for three hours and stars were visible in the sky. While it was still dark Jesus said, **"Father, into Your hands I commit My spirit." Having said this, He breathed His last**. (Luke 23:46). Therefore, Jesus died on the cross when it was dark as night. Then after Jesus died on the cross it became light as day again until sunset (6:00 P.M.).

Since the Jews may count a part of a day as a whole,[12:2] the dark as night when Jesus died on the cross and the light as day after Jesus died until sunset count as a sign to Israel of the first night and day of the death of Jesus. Jesus was placed in the tomb before sunset during the first day; therefore, He was in the tomb in the heart of the earth the first day before sunset. Then the night after sunset and the day of the Passover that Jesus was in the tomb count as the second night and a day that was a sign to Israel. The night after the Passover and the morning of the first day of the week that Jesus was in the tomb before He rose from the dead count as the third night and a day that was a sign to Israel.

12:2 Rabbi Eleazar ben Azariah, a late first century rabbi, is quoted in regard to a part of a day as a whole, "A day and night are an Onah and the portion of an Onah is as the whole of it."[12:3]
Jerusalem Talmud: Shabbath ix. 3; and Babylonian Talmud: Pesahim 4

12:3 Harold W. Hoehner *Chronological Aspects of the Life of Christ* (Academie Books, Grand Rapids MI.: Zondervan 1977) p. 74

As High Priest Jesus was not crucified for his own sins. He did not need to offer a sacrifice for Himself before entering the Most Holy Place as Aaronic high priests needed to enter a sacrifice for their own sins before entering the Holy of Holies.
Hebrews 7:26-27
26 For such a High Priest was fitting for us, *who is* holy, harmless, undefiled, separate from sinners, and has become higher than the heavens; 27 who does not need daily, as those high priests, to offer up sacrifices, first for His own sins, and then for the people's, for this He did once for all when He offered up Himself.

God is so holy that he cannot bear to look upon sin that has not been judged. Habakkuk 1:13 says, **"*You are* of purer eyes than to behold evil, and cannot look on wickedness."**

Because God is holy, he cannot compromise with sin; sin must be judged.

The crucifixion of Jesus was atoning and sacrificial

The crucifixion of Jesus was sacrificial
Jesus prophesied his own crucifixion and resurrection before it happened, referring to Himself as the Son of Man.
Mark 9:31
31 For He taught His disciples and said to them, "The Son of Man is being betrayed into the hands of men, and they will kill Him. And after He is killed, He will rise the third day."

It was not a matter of God rescuing a righteous man from the cross; it was a matter of the only righteous one sacrificed on the cross for the sins of the many that believe in him.
John 10:17-18
17 "Therefore my Father loves Me, because I lay down My life that I may take it again. 18 No one takes it from Me, but I lay it down of Myself. I have power to lay it down, and I have power to take it again. This commandment I have received from My Father."

The crucifixion of Jesus was atoning; the atoning death of Jesus fulfills Leviticus 17:11
Leviticus 17:11
11 **For the life of the flesh *is* in the blood, and I have given it to you upon the altar to make atonement for your souls; for it *is* the blood *that* makes atonement for the soul.**

When Old Testament saints gave animal sacrifices in the Temple, God was looking forward to the day of the atoning sacrificial death of the Messiah 'Christ' on the cross.

Now, there is no longer a need for the sacrifice of animals because the atoning sacrifice of the Messiah 'Christ' is once for all.
Hebrews 9:12
12 **Not with the blood of goats and calves, but with His own blood He entered the Most Holy Place once for all, having obtained eternal redemption.**

The Levitical sacrifices and the tabernacle in the Jerusalem Temple are mere physical copies and shadows of a far greater spiritual reality

There is a Temple in heaven made without hands. Revelation 11:19 speaks of the Temple in heaven. Although, it speaks of the Temple during the time of the future Great Tribulation, it shows that there is a Temple in heaven with an Ark of His covenant inside.

Revelation 11:19
19 **Then the temple of God was opened in heaven, and the ark of His covenant was seen in His temple. And there were lightnings, noises, thunderings, an earthquake and great hail.**

After His atoning sacrificial death on the cross Jesus presented himself before God the Father in heaven.
Hebrews 9:24
24 **For Christ has not entered the holy places made with hands, *which are* copies of the true, but into heaven itself, now to appear in the presence of God for us.**

Hebrews 9:11-12

11 But Christ came *as* **High Priest of the good things to come, with the greater and more perfect tabernacle not made with hands, that is not of this creation. 12 Not with the blood of goats and calves, but with His own blood He entered the Most Holy Place once for all, having obtained eternal redemption.**

When Levitical sacrifices were made, God looked forward to the atoning sacrificial death of the Messiah, the Ruler, Jesus on the cross. Since the atoning sacrificial death of the Messiah, the Ruler, Jesus has been accomplished and He has presented himself before God the Father in heaven, now there is no longer need for Levitical sacrifices in an earthly Temple.

All mankind except Jesus has sinned and fallen short of the glory of God. Sin causes enmity between a sinner and God who is a holy God.

All mankind has fallen short of the glory of God. Romans 3:23 says, **"For all have sinned and fall short of the glory of God."**

1 John 1:8 says, **"If we say that we have no sin, we deceive ourselves, and the truth is not in us."**

We sin in our hearts and by our deeds quite often, whereas just one sin is enough to cause enmity between God and a man or woman. Because God is a holy God, sin must be judged. A holy God cannot compromise with sin. Romans 6:23a says, **"For the wages of sin is death, but the gift of God is eternal life in Christ Jesus our Lord.**

God is love.

God provided Himself as the atonement for sin through the atoning sacrificial death of Jesus Christ on the cross. John 3:16 says, **"For God so loved the world that He gave His only begotten Son, that whoever believes in Him should not perish but have everlasting life."**

1 John 1:7b says, **"The blood of Jesus Christ His Son cleanses us from all sin."**

Chapter 13

The resurrection of Jesus from the dead on the Day of Firstfruits of the barley harvest

As Jesus was placed in the tomb Mary Magdalene and the other Mary observed where He was laid, (Matthew 27:61). The women went home and prepared spices and oil, then rested on the Sabbath, (Luke 23:56). The next day after the Day of Preparation [Day of the Passover] the chief priests spoke to Pilate requesting that he set a guard at the tomb lest his disciples steal his body and claim he had risen. Pilate said, "You have a guard," so they set their own guards at the tomb, (Matthew 27:64-67). On the morning of the first day of the week the women came to see the tomb.

Matthew 28:2-4

2 And behold, there was a great earthquake; for an angel of the Lord descended from heaven, and came and rolled back the stone from the door, and sat on it. 3 His countenance was like lightning, and his clothing white as snow. 4 And the guards shook for fear of him, and became like dead *men.*

When the women came to the tomb; they found the stone rolled away. When they went in the tomb; they did not find the body of Jesus. As the women were perplexed, behold, two men in shining garments stood by them and said to them.

Luke 24:5-7

5b "Why do you seek the living among the dead? 6 He is not here, but is risen! Remember how He spoke to you when He was still in Galilee. 7 Saying, 'The son of man must be delivered into the hands of sinful men, and be crucified, and the third day rise again.'"

When Mary Magdalene, Joanna, Mary *the mother of* James, and the other women with them told the eleven disciples, their words seemed like idle tales to them, (Luke 24:8-12). Peter and the other disciple, who Jesus loved, went out and ran to the tomb together. The other disciple ran faster and looking in saw the linen clothes. Then Peter went in and saw the handkerchief that had been around His head folded by itself. Then the other disciple went in and he saw and believed. Then they went home, (John 20:3-10).

But Mary Magdalene remained outside the tomb weeping and as she stooped to look inside the tomb, she saw two angels in white.

John 20:13

13 Then they said to her. "Woman, why are you weeping?" She said to them, "Because they have taken away my Lord, and I do not know where they have laid Him."

Then she saw Jesus and supposing Him to be the gardener she asked him. Jesus spoke her name and she realized it was him.

John 20:17

17 Jesus said to her, "Do not cling to me, for I have not yet ascended to My Father; but go to My brethren and say to them, 'I am ascending to My Father and your Father, and to My God and your God.'"

Then that same day, the first day of the week, at evening the disciples were together (except for Thomas) and the doors were shut. Jesus stood among them and He showed them His hands and His side, then the disciples were glad, (John 20:19-20).

John 20:21-22

21 So Jesus said to them again, "Peace to you! As the father has sent Me, I also send you." 22 And when He had said this, He breathed on *them*, and said to them, "Receive the Holy Spirit."

When the disciples told Thomas that they had seen the Lord, he did not believe them. Then eight days later as the disciples were in the room Jesus appeared among them again and Thomas believed.

Over a period of forty days Jesus appeared to many people in various places and He gave them the great commission to preach the gospel.

Mark 16:15

15 And He said to them, "Go into all the world and preach the gospel to every creature."

As they were together Jesus commanded them not to depart from Jerusalem, but wait for the promise of the Father, (Acts 1:4).

Acts 1:9-11

9 Now when He had spoken these things, while they watched, He was taken up, and a cloud received Him out of their sight. 10 And while they looked steadfastly toward heaven as He went up, behold, two men stood by them in white apparel, 11 who also said, "Men of Galilee, why do you stand gazing up into heaven? This *same* Jesus, who was taken from you into heaven, will so come in like manner as you saw Him go into heaven."

Jesus rose from the dead on the Day of Firstfruits.

According to Leviticus 23:9-14, a sheaf of the firstfruits of the grain harvest is to be taken from the field and waved by the priests before the Lord to be accepted on their behalf. It is to be waved on the day after the Sabbath.

The resurrection of Jesus from the dead was on the day after the Sabbath, the first day of the week. The Day of Firstfruits is a day after the Sabbath and since the Passover was on a Sabbath Day that year, the Day of Firstfruits was the day after the Passover. The resurrection of Jesus from the dead is the Firstfruit of those in Christ that will be resurrected at the time of his appearing.

1 Corinthians 15:20-23

20 But now Christ is risen from the dead, *and* has become the firstfruits of those who have fallen asleep. 21 For since by man *came* death, by man also *came* the resurrection of the dead. 22 For as in Adam all die, even so in Christ all shall be made alive. 23 But each one in his own order: Christ the firstfruits, afterward those *who are* Christ's at His coming.

Regeneration

On the same day that Jesus rose from the dead, the disciples were in a room with the door locked. Jesus came to them, showed them His wounds from His crucifixion, and they believed in Him. Upon their confession of belief, Jesus breathed on them, and said, **"Receive the Holy Spirit."** The disciples that Jesus breathed upon are the firstfruits of the indwelling of the Holy Spirit within those in Christ upon the earth. The disciples that Jesus breathed upon are a type of born-again Christians that have the indwelling of the Holy Spirit. Earlier Jesus had spoken about being born again.

John 3:5-6

5 Jesus answered, "Most assuredly, I say to you, unless one is born of water and the Spirit, he cannot enter the kingdom of God. 6 That which is born of the flesh is flesh, and that which is born of the Spirit is spirit.

"Born of water and the Spirit" refers to being born of the Spirit with the quality of the washing of water.

All of mankind born of the flesh after Adam have sinned and fallen short of the glory of God. Those in Christ are born again of the Holy Spirit after Jesus Christ, the sinless second Adam, who died on the cross for the sins of those who receive him.

The apostle Paul expresses it as a new creation in Christ.
2 Cor. 5:17 **Therefore, if anyone *is* in Christ, *he is* a new creation; old things have passed away; behold, all things have become new.**
The Holy Spirit dwells in Christians and all Christians are the Temple of God.
1 Cor. 3:16 **Do you not know that you are the temple of God and *that* the Spirit of God dwells in you?**

Justification

Two popular short definitions are: "grace is unmerited favor" and "justification is just as if you hadn't sinned." However, in the case of justification that is not quite completely correct because justification is so much more than just as if you hadn't sinned. Justification or righteousness goes beyond the law under which mankind cannot fully attain righteousness.

Ephesians 2:8-9
8 For by grace you have been saved through faith, and that not of yourselves; *it is* the gift of God, 9 not of works, lest anyone should boast.

Faith is the means; the source of righteousness is God
Romans 4:20-22 speaks of Abraham that he believed God and, **"It was accounted to him for righteousness."**
Then in Rom. 4:23-25 it is applied to Christians. **"Now it was not written for his sake alone that it was imputed to him, 24 but also for us. It shall be imputed to us who believe in Him who raised up Jesus our Lord from the dead, 25 who was delivered up because of our offenses, and was raised because of our justification."**

Through repentance and faith in the atoning sacrificial death and resurrection from the dead of Jesus the Christ 'Messiah,' the believer is pardoned, acquitted, the righteousness of Christ is imputed to the believer and God declares the believer to be righteous in His sight.

If one were merely pardoned and acquitted, that one would still lack a positive standing in the sight of God.

Adoption

The believer in Christ is made a member of God's family, and becomes a fellow heir with Christ.

John 1:12

12. **But as many as received Him, to them gave He power to become the sons of God,** *even* **to them that believe on His name.**

The Interlinear Greek- English New Testament, The Reverend Alferd Marshall (London, WI.: Samuel Bagster and Sons Lim., 1958)

Rom. 8:14-17

14. **For as many as are led by the Spirit of God, these are sons of God. 15 For you did not receive the spirit of bondage again to fear, but received the Spirit of adoption by whom we cry out, "Abba, Father." 16 The Spirit Himself bears witness with our spirit that we are children of God, 17 and if children, then heirs—heirs of God and joint heirs with Christ, if indeed we suffer with *Him*, that we may also be glorified together.**

Adoption is present and future. The full extent of adoption is fulfilled when the Lord Jesus Christ returns and those in Christ receive resurrected glorified bodies like Jesus after he rose from the dead.

Romans 8:23

23 **Not only *that* but we also who have the firstfruits of the spirit, even we ourselves groan within ourselves, eagerly waiting for the adoption, the redemption of our body.**

Chapter 14

Extrabiblical evidence of a red moon in the evening on the day Jesus was crucified

Following the resurrection of Jesus from the dead, He spoke to His disciples on several occasions during a period of forty days before He ascended to heaven. Before Jesus ascended to heaven, He commanded His disciples not to depart from Jerusalem, but to wait for the promise of the Father. Jesus told His disciples that John baptized with water, but you shall be baptized with the Holy Spirit not many days from now. About one hundred and twenty disciples gathered in the upper room in one accord in prayer and supplication.

On the Day of Pentecost, suddenly there came a sound from heaven as of a rushing mighty wind. Then tongues of fire sat upon each of them in the upper room and they were filled with the Holy Spirit and begin to speak in other languages beyond their understanding as the Spirit gave them utterance. A crowd of people from many diverse places that were in Jerusalem for the celebration of the Day of Pentecost heard those that were filled with the Holy Spirit praise God in their own language. Peter stood and spoke to the crowd that had gathered saying, **"This is what was spoken of by the prophet Joel."** Then as described in Acts 2:17-21, Peter spoke the prophecy of Joel to the crowd.

Acts 2:17-21

17 'And it shall come to pass in the last days, says God, That I will pour out my Spirit on all flesh; Your sons and your daughters shall prophesy, Your young men shall see visions, Your old men shall dream dreams. 18 And on My manservants and on My maidservants I will pour out My Spirit in those days and they shall prophesy. 19 I will show wonders in heaven above and signs in the earth beneath: blood and fire and vapor and smoke. 20 The sun shall be turned into darkness, and the moon into blood, before the coming of the great and awesome day of the Lord. 21 And it shall come to pass that whoever calls on the name of the Lord shall be saved.'

The Old Testament passage written in Hebrew by the prophet Joel that Peter spoke of is in Joel 2:28-32. **"The sun shall be turned into darkness, and the moon into blood,"** (Joel 2:31).

The Day of Pentecost is on the fiftieth day after the Passover. It celebrates the end of the barley harvest and the Firstfruits of the wheat harvest. It is the Feast of Harvest when two loaves made from newly ground grain were presented before the Lord. On the Day of Pentecost, those in the upper room that were baptized with the Holy Spirit were the Firstfruits of the infilling of the Holy Spirit in Christians.

There was a red moon in the evening on the day that Jesus was crucified

Joel 2:31 speaks of the sun being turned into darkness, and the moon into blood. Peter spoke on the Day of Pentecost to the crowd of these things being the fulfilment of a prophecy of Joel.

The gospels speak of an extended period of darkness of three hours from the sixth hour until the ninth hour on the day Jesus was crucified. Since, dawn is at 6:00 A.M. in Jerusalem during the time of the Passover, the sixth hour of the day is at 12:00 P.M. (noon), and the ninth hour of the day is at 3:00 P.M.

Joel's prophesy of darkness was fulfilled. Was the moon turned to blood after sunset that same day? The answer is yes. On the day Jesus was crucified, there was darkness for three hours during the day and after sunset as the moon rose it was red.

We know that the moon appears red during an eclipse of the moon when the moon is exactly on the opposite side of the earth from the sun. When the moon is in the shadow of the earth, some of the light from the sun is refracted by the earth's atmosphere onto the moon. Blue light waves are a shorter wave length than red light waves. The shorter length blue light waves are absorbed by the atmosphere to a greater degree than the longer red light waves with the result that the light refracted upon the moon during an eclipse of the moon is mostly red.

April 3, 33 A.D. Julian, which was a Friday, has been firmly established as the date of the crucifixion of Jesus by astrological calculations and April 3, 33 A.D. Julian corresponds to Nisan 14, 3793 Hebrew

There have been several persons calculating the appearance of a red moon during the time of the Passover while Pontius Pilate was the Roman procurator/prefect of Judea, 26-36 A.D., since Pilate was the Roman procurator/prefect of Judea when Jesus was crucified. The most accurate calculation to this date was done by Oxford astrophysicist Graeme Waddington at the request of his friend, Colin J. Humphreys.

The U. S. National Aeronautics and Space Administration did a precise study of the orbit of the moon and the rotation of the earth in order to facilitate an accurate landing on the moon.

Based on NASA studies of the orbit of the moon and the rotation of the earth, Graeme Waddington calculated that there was only one eclipse of the moon at the time of the Passover during the time period of 26-36 A.D. "It was Friday, April 3, AD 33."[14:1] The total eclipse happened before the moon appeared over the horizon and as the Jews were watching for the moon that began the day of the Passover, it was already a red moon.

An article by Colin J. Humphreys and Oxford astrophysicist Graeme Waddington passed a peer review and was published in Nature Magazine in 1983.

Colin J. Humphreys and W. G. Waddington, 'Dating the Crucifixion' *Nature* 306 (1983) pp. 743-6

In the article the red moon is diagrammed as a waning partial red moon as it first appeared over the horizon of Jerusalem.

Later Colin J. Humphrey wrote a book about the last supper, which mentions the red moon.

Colin J. Humphreys, *THE MYSTERY of THE LAST SUPPER. Reconstructing the Final Days of Jesus,* (Cambridge University Press. 2011)

14:1. Colin J. Humphreys, *THE MYSTERY of THE LAST SUPPER. Reconstructing the Final Days of Jesus,* (Cambridge University Press. 2011) p. 90

Chapter 15
Extrabiblical evidence of darkness during the day on the day Jesus was crucified

Matthew 27:45, Mark 15:33, and Luke 23:44 speak of darkness from the sixth hour, which would be at noon, until the ninth hour, which would be at 3 PM, on the day Jesus was crucified.

On the day of Pentecost Peter quotes a prophesy of Joel as being fulfilled that says, **"The sun shall be turned into darkness, and the moon into blood,"** (Joel 2:31).

By means of astronomical calculations, there is extrabiblical evidence that there was a red moon just after sunset on the day Jesus was crucified.

There is also extrabiblical evidence for darkness during the daytime on the day Jesus was crucified.

Julius Africanus was a man of many diverse abilities. He wrote in Greek and also knew Hebrew and Latin. He was an ambassador to Rome on behalf of Emmaus. The Emperor Alexander Sever (222-235 A.D.) was so impressed by his knowledge, he entrusted Africanus with the building of his library at the Pantheon in Rome. Africanus had a military background and wrote about military tactics.

At some point in his life he converted from paganism to being a Christian. In his *Chronographiai* in five volumes, he set about the task of systemizing the chronology of the Bible with profane writers. That task led to Africanus investigating the writings of Thallus and Phlegon. In (XIII.2), Africanus speaks of Thallus and Phlegon (as historians among other well-known historians at that time, who are even known at the present time) in the context of using the Olympiads for dating.

Julius Africanus *Chronographiai* (XIII.2)

"And after 70 years of captivity, Cyrus became king of the Persians at the time of the 55th Olympiad, as may be ascertained from the *Bibliothecae* of Diodorus and the histories of Thallus and Castor, and also from Polybius and Phlegon, and others besides these, who have made the Olympiads a subject of study. For the date is a matter of agreement among them all."[15:1]

In (XIII.3) Africanus speaks of Thallus as one who records Syrian affairs in the context of using Attic time-reckoning as the standard for recording affairs.

Julius Africanus *Chronographiai* (XIII.3)

"For these things are also recorded by the Athenian historians Hellanicus and Philochorus, who record Attic affairs, and by Castor and Thallus, who record Syrian affairs, and by Diodorus, who writes a universal history in his Bibliothecae; and by Alexander Polyhistr, and by some of our own time, yet more carefully."[15:2]

In *Antiquities* 18.167, Josephus speaks of a certain Thallus who lent a million drachmas to Herod Agrippa, which apparently is the same Thallus that Africanus speaks of, since the time and location fit. Such a friend of Herod would most likely not be a Christian.

Thallus and Phlegen, who were not Christians, reported about the darkness during the day in their writings; however, they attributed the darkness to an eclipse of the sun. Africanus disputes that interpretation because there cannot be an eclipse of the sun during the time when there is nearly a full moon.

Julius Africanus *Chronographiai* (XVIII.1)

"As to his works severally, and His cures effected upon body and soul, and the mysteries of His doctrine, and the resurrection from the dead, these have been most authoritatively set forth by His disciples and apostles before us. On the whole world there passed a most fearful darkness; and the rocks were rent by an earthquake, and many places in Judea and other districts were thrown down.

This darkness Thallus, in the third book of his *History,* calls, as appears to me to be without reason, an eclipse of the sun. For the Hebrews celebrate the Passover on the 14th day according to the moon, and the passion of our Savior falls on the day before the Passover, but an eclipse of the sun takes place only when the moon comes under the sun. And it cannot happen at any other time but in the interval between the first day of the new moon and the last of the old, that is, at their junction: how then should an eclipse be supposed to happen when the moon is almost diametrically opposite the sun? Let opinion pass however; let it carry the majority with it; and let this portent of the world be deemed an eclipse of the sun, like others a portent only to the eye. Phlegon records that, in the time of Tiberius Caesar, at full noon, there was a full eclipse of the sun from the sixth hour to the ninth—manifestly that one of which we speak. But what has an eclipse in common with an earthquake, the renting of rocks, and the resurrection of the dead, and so great a perturbation throughout the universe? Surely no such event as this is recorded for a long period. But it was a darkness induced by God, because the Lord happened then to suffer. And calculation makes out that the period of 70 weeks, as noted in Daniel, is completed at this time."[15:3]

Sextus Julius Africanus had direct knowledge of Thallus' writing; he referred specifically to Thallus' third book of *History*. Julius Africanus argued against the interpretation by Thallus in his third book of *History* that the darkness was an eclipse of the sun. Julius Africanus argued against it as an eclipse of the sun because during the Passover the moon is on the opposite side of the earth than when there is an eclipse of the sun. Julius Africanus gave an accurate explanation of when eclipses of the sun occur; they occur during the interval between the new moon and the old moon when the moon is directly in line between the earth and the sun.

Phlegon wrote that there was a great eclipse of the sun and a great earthquake. The early Christians believed that the darkness and earthquake that happened during the crucifixion of Jesus was a miracle. Julius Africanus also challenged Phlegon's interpretation that it was an eclipse of the sun as he questioned, what has an eclipse in common with an earthquake? No such combination of events has been recorded before.

The early church historian Eusebius* of Caesarea, also set out to write a chronology. Eusebius had knowledge of the 13th book of Phlegon of Tralles for in his *Chronicon II*, Eusebius quotes Phlegon's 13th book concerning a great eclipse of the sun and an earthquake. The passage in Eusebius' *Chronicon II* that quotes Phlegon's 13th book that speaks of a great eclipse of the sun and a great earthquake is on the following page.
*Nicknamed Pamphili (son of Pamphilus) after his teacher Saint Pamphilus of Caesarea, who was martyred in 310 A.D. during the Diocletian persecution; however, often referred to as Eusebius Pamphilus

Eusebius of Caesarea, *Chronicon II*
(quoting from Phlegon's 13th book of *Olympiades he Chronika*)

Ἰησοῦς ὁ Χριστὸς ὁ Υἱὸς τοῦ Θεοῦ, ὁ Κύριος ἡμῶν, κατὰ τὰς περὶ αὐτοῦ προφητείας ἐπὶ τὸ πάθος προῄει ἔτους ιθ τῆς Τιβερίου βασιλείας. Καθ' ὃν καιρὸν καὶ ἐν ἄλλοις μὲν Ἑλληνικοῖς ὑπομνήμασιν εὕρομεν ἱστορούμενα κατὰ λέξιν ταῦτα· "Ὁ ἥλιος ἐξέλιπε· Βιθυνία ἐσείσθη· Νικαίας τὰ πολλὰ ἔπεσεν·" ἃ καὶ συνᾴδει τοῖς περὶ τὸ πάθος τοῦ Σωτῆρος ἡμῶν συμβεβηκόσι. Γράφει δὲ καὶ Φλέγων ὁ τὰς ὀλυμπιάδας (sc. συναγαγὼν) περὶ τῶν αὐτῶν ἐν τῳ τριεκαιδεκάτῳ ῥήμασιν αὐτοῖς τάδε· τῷ δ ἔτει τῆς σβ Ὀλυμπιάδος ἐγένετο ἔκλειψις ἡλίου μεγίστη τῶν ἐγνωρισμένων πρότερον, καὶ νὺξ ὥρα ἕκτη τῆς ἡμέρας ἐγένετο, ὥστε καὶ ἀστέρας ἐν οὐρανῷ φανῆναι· σεισμός τε μέγας κατὰ Βιθυνίαν γενόμενος τὰ πολλὰ Νικαίας κατεστρέψατο.   Syncellus p. 324 D. ex Euseb. Chron. II p. 148 Sch. (via) Otto Keller, ed. *Rerum Naturalium Scriptores Graeci Minores, vol. I; Phlegon, XVII.* (Leipzig: Teubner, 1877) p. 101

Translation of Greek on page 101
Jesus the Christ, the Son of God, our Lord, according to the prophecies concerning him about his suffering *that* originate from the 19th year of the Tiberius kingdom. At that time and in others, on the one hand, in Greek records we found stories *and* according to *them* saying the same thing, "The sun having forsook, Bithynia being shook, many things of Nicaea fell down," and that it agrees to having had happened concerning the suffering of our Savior. And on the other hand, Phlegon in the Olympiads writes (having gathered) concerning them in his 13th book this, "In the 4th year in the 202nd Olympiad, it became the greatest eclipse of the sun having been known before, and it became night the sixth hour of the day, and so that stars in heaven to have shined. A great earthquake having happened at Bithynia *and* many things of Nicaea were thrown down."

Translation of Greek on page 101 by the author of this book, Douglas Ophus

Eusebius of Caesarea was well versed in the dating method according to the Olympiads. He refers to Jesus suffering in the 19th year of the Tiberius Kingdom (33 A.D.) and that it agrees with the 4th year of the 202nd Olympiad. The 4th year of the 202nd Olympiad would have been from the summer of 32 A.D. to the summer of 33 A.D., which includes when Jesus was crucified April 3, 33 A.D.

The darkness cannot be explained as an eclipse of the sun because it was during the time when the moon was nearly full, and it cannot be explained as a dust storm because the stars were visible in the sky. Furthermore, the darkness occurred at the sixth hour and there was an earthquake, both events in agreement with the gospels.

There are three things that indicate that Phlegon's writing is based on an observation of the event of the darkness independent of the gospels.

First, there is the misinterpretation that the darkness was caused by an eclipse of the sun. The early Christians believed it was a miracle that happened during the crucifixion of Jesus; they argued against it as an eclipse of the sun because during the Passover the moon is on the opposite side of the earth than when there is an eclipse of the sun.

Second, Eusebius speaks of Greeks recording stories that are independent of the Bible speaking of Ὁ ἥλιος ἐξέλιπε * 'the sun forsook or vanished' and while it was dark as night there was a great earthquake. An incident such as that would be remembered a long time.

Third, the statement of Phlegon saying, "Stars in heaven to have shined" cannot be attributed to a quote from one of the gospels because the gospels do not mention stars in heaven to have shined. Therefore, it is an assertion made independent of the gospels as its source.

Sextus Julius Africanus mentions Phlegon along with several other ancient historians that were not known to be Christians. That indicates that the assertion made by Phlegon, "Stars in heaven to have shined" was based on an observation of the actual event written independent of the gospels.

* ἐξέλιπε 'It forsook' as if it vanished from sight, aorist active indicative 3rd person singular of ἐκλείπω 'I forsake.' (The aorist verb form is used for wholistic action).

Chapter 15 Extrabiblical evidence of darkness during the day on the day Jesus was crucified, quotations

The ANTE-NICENE FATHERS Translations of *The writings of the Fathers down to A.D. 325,* The Rev. Alexander Roberts, D. D. and James Donaldson, LL. D. editors; AMERICAN REPRINT OF THE EDINBURGH EDITION; Volume VI.
(THE CHRISTIAN LITERATURE COMPANY, N. Y., 1890)
And
(WM. B. EERDMANS PUBLISHING COMPANY Grand Rapids, MI. Photolithoprinted by Cushing – Malloy, Inc. Ann Arbor, MI. 1957)

15:1. Ibid., P. 133

15:2. Ibid., P. 133

15:3. Ibid., P. 136 & 137

Flavius Josephus was a Jew that was an eye witness to the destruction of Jerusalem and the Temple by the Roman army in 70 A.D. The Romans conquered Jotapata in Galilee at the time Josephus was in charge of its defense and during the massacre Josephus entered a pit where there were about 40 people. While he was there, he had a dream that God wanted him to write about the things that were happening. His surrender to the Romans was preceded by a death pact involving the drawing of lots (not to be confused with the one that happened at Masada) where Josephus depended upon divine providence for the outcome. Josephus is the primary source for the description of the destruction of Jerusalem and the Temple. It is interesting that aside from a little by Tacitus, without *A History of the Jewish Wars* by Josephus very little would be known about the destruction of Jerusalem and the Temple.

Chapter 16
The Romans sacked the city of Jerusalem and destroyed the Temple in 70 A.D. Julian

Daniel 9:26b
And the people of the Prince who is to come shall destroy the city and the sanctuary. The end of it *shall be* with a flood.

When the seventy sevens prophecy was told to Daniel by the angel Gabriel, the Temple was destroyed. It presupposes that the Temple will be rebuilt again. Then after seven sevens and sixty-two sevens after the decree to rebuild Jerusalem with streets and a wall the Temple will be destroyed again. Then the Temple will be rebuilt again during the seventieth seven so that the daily sacrifice may be taken away and the abomination that causes desolation may be committed.

In outer words: the people of the ruler who will come will destroy the city [Jerusalem] and the sanctuary [Temple].

It will be the people of the ruler to come that will destroy the city and the sanctuary, not the ruler himself, who will come later. This prophecy has been fulfilled; it is a well known historical fact that the Roman army destroyed Jerusalem and the Temple, and the accepted date for when it happened is 70 A.D. Julian.

The future ruler that will come at a later time is "**He**" that is spoken of in Daniel 9:25 **He will make a covenant with many for one seven**. That seven years will be the seventieth seven years in the prophecy; however, before that a period of **desolations has been decreed**. The number of desolations and the duration of the desolations is not defined in the prophecy. As such, there is a period of indefinite time in the counting of the sevens, often referred to as a time gap.

Then after the time gap, the seventieth seven years will begin when the covenant with many participants for seven years is made.

Signs from God that the people of Jerusalem had ignored before the Roman army's siege on Jerusalem.

The Jewish historian Flavius Josephus is a primary source for the description of the Roman army's destruction of the city of Jerusalem and the temple. In his writing, *A History of The Jewish Wars,* he was an eyewitness to the part about the destruction of the city of Jerusalem and the Temple.

During the Roman army's siege on Jerusalem, Josephus spoke from outside the wall of the city saying that before the attack they had listened to a false prophet and had ignored the signs from God.

Book VI Ch, IV

A peasant named Jesus, son of Ananias,[*] who came during a peaceful time to the Feast of the Tabernacles four years before the war of the Jews with the Romans and began to cry aloud, "A voice from the east, a voice from the west, a voice from the four winds, a voice against Jerusalem and the holy house, a voice against the bridegrooms and the brides, and a voice against this whole people!"[16:1] He went about the streets saying, "Woe, woe to Jerusalem" and even though he was whipped with stripes he kept on for seven years and five months until one day he said, "Woe, woe to myself also" as there came a stone from an engine and killed him.[16:2]

There were other signs too, "A star resembling a sword which stood over the city, and a comet, that continued a whole year."[16:3]

At a time before the war at "the Feast of Unleavened Bread, on the eighth day of the month Xanthicus [Nisan], and at the ninth hour of the day, so great a light shone round the altar and the holy house that it appeared to be bright as daytime; which light lasted for half an hour."[16:4] To the unskilled it seemed a good sign, but the scribes interpreted it "as to portend those events that followed immediately upon it."[16:5] "At the same festival also, a heifer, as she was led by the high priest to be sacrificed, brought forth a lamb in the midst of the Temple. Moreover, the Eastern Gate of the inner [court of the] Temple, which was of brass, and vastly heavy"[16:6] "opened of its own accord about the sixth hour of the night."[16:7]

* not Jesus of Nazareth in the Bible over three decades earlier.

Beside these a few days after the feast on the twenty first day of the month of Artemisius [Iyyar], "Before sunsetting, chariots and troops of soldiers in their armor were seen running about among the clouds, and surrounding of cities."[16:8]

And a very theologically significant event occurred, "at that feast which we call Pentecost, as the priests were going by night into the inner [court of the] Temple, as their custom was, to perform their sacred ministrations, they said that, in the first place, they felt a quaking, and heard a great noise, and after that they heard a sound as of a great multitude, saying 'Let us remove hence.'"[16:9]

That is similar to an earlier time when the prophet Ezekiel saw the Cherubim leaving Solomon's Temple before the Lord allowed Nebuchadnezzar's army to destroy it.

Ezekiel 10:18-19a

18 **Then the glory of the Lord departed from the threshold of the temple and stood over the cherubim.** 19a **And the cherubim lifted their wings and mounted up from the earth in my sight.**

The Feast of Pentecost when the priest heard the voices of a multitude saying that they were leaving this place, must have been a Pentecost at least a year previous to the Roman attack on Jerusalem because the Roman attack occurred during the Feast of Unleavened Bread, which begins 50 days before the Feast of Pentecost.

The destruction of the Jerusalem Temple is a testimony to the sufficiency of the atoning sacrifice of Christ that once for all time fulfilled the sacrifices performed in the Temple.

The atoning sacrifice of Jesus the Christ on the cross fulfilled the sacrifices performed in the Temple for all people who believe in Him. Hebrews 10:10, **By that will we have been sanctified through the offering of the body of Christ once *for* all.** Now there is no longer a need for sacrifices to be performed in the Temple.

Those that repent and receive Christ for themselves are born again with the indwelling of the Holy Spirit. Christians with the indwelling of the Holy Spirit all together are the Temple of God.
1 Cor. 3:16
16 Know ye not that ye are the temple of God, and that the Spirit of God dwelleth in you?
The Interlinear Greek- English New Testament, The Reverend Alferd Marshall (London: Samuel Bagster and Sons Limited, 1958)

Modern English does not distinguish between singular 'you' and plural 'you.' However, sometimes in Biblical theology that distinction is important; therefore, some versions of the Bible use 'ye' to represent 'you' in the plural. Thus, 1 Corinthians 3:16 teaches that the Spirit of God dwells in 'you' individually and that along with other Christians 'ye' corporately are the Temple of God.

The atoning sacrifice of Christ on the cross once for all completed the need for sacrifices performed in the Temple, yet sacrifices continued to be performed in the Temple until the gospel was preached to those that performed sacrifices in the Temple. There was an overlap where sacrifices were performed in the Temple while the gospel was being preached to those that performed sacrifices in the Temple until a certain time when the gospel had been sufficiently preached to those that performed sacrifices in the Temple.

Since God had moved His residence from the Temple building to indwell in His people, at a certain time after the gospel had been preached to those who performed sacrifices in the Temple, the Lord spoke to the priests in the Temple through the holy multitude saying that they were leaving this place.

That was because according to Hebrews 10:4, **For it is not possible that the blood of bulls and goats could take away sins.** When sacrifices were made in the Temple the Lord looked forward to when **the Messiah will be cut off, but not for Himself**, and that was when Jesus, who is the Messiah, was crucified on the cross for those that believe in Him.

The glory of the Lord departed from the Temple. The enemy took opportunity and **the people of the prince who *is* to come shall destroy the city and the sanctuary.**

The destruction of the city of Jerusalem and the Temple by the Roman army

In his *Jewish Antiquities*, written after *The Jewish Wars,* the Jewish historian Flavius Josephus blames Procurator Gessius Florus that he compelled the Jews to go to war with the Romans. In some places in his description, Josephus is obviously pandering to the Romans, especially in the case of Titus.

The Following is a summary with excerpts from *"The Works of Flavius Josephus: A History of The Jewish Wars"* as translated by William Whiston.

Gessius Florus was a corrupt procurator and he mistreated the people wanting them to rebel in order to cover up his corruption. Book II Ch. XIV

"He [procurator Gessius Florus] indeed thought it but a petty offense to get money out of a single person; so he spoiled whole cities, and did almost publicly proclaim it all the country over, that they had liberty given to them to turn robbers, upon this condition, that he might go shares with them in the spoils."[16:10]

"He [Florus] expected that, if the peace continued, he should have the Jews for his accusers before Caesar: but that if he could procure them to make a revolt, he should divert their laying lesser crimes to his charge, by a misery that was so much greater; he therefore did every day augment their calamities, in order to induce them to rebellion."[16:11]

The Jews did not want to rebel against the Romans, but rather have Gessius Florus the Procurator sent by Rome replaced. Book II Ch. XVII

The Jews requested that King Agrippa send ambassadors to Rome to appeal to Nero to replace Florus. "He [Agrippa] attempted to persuade the multitude to obey Florus, until Caesar should send one to succeed him; but they were hereby more provoked, and cast reproaches upon the king, and got him excluded out of the city; nay, some of the seditious [rebels] had the impudence to throw stones at him."[16:12]

The 66 A.D. Jewish 'rebel' rebellion against Roman rule

The war Josephus was speaking of began in August, 66 A.D. In *The Jewish Wars* Josephus speaks of a Jewish rebellion committed by certain rebels on the day of the festival of wood-carrying.

At the festival of Xylophory, it was the custom for everyone to bring wood for the altar that there might be sufficient fuel for the fire to be always burning. The opposite party had been excluded from observing that part of it. As they joined together the Sicarii crowded in among them. Sicarii "was the name for such robbers as had under their bosom's swords called sicae,"[16:13] they overpowered the king's soldiers and drove them out of the upper city. "The others then set fire to the house of Ananias the high priest, and to the palaces of Agrippa and Bernice; after which they carried the fire to the place where the archives were deposited, and made haste to burn the contracts belonging to their creditors, and thereby dissolve their obligations for paying their debts."[16:14]

There may have been death records there too that would have also been burned. In the following paragraph, Josephus writes, "But on the next day, which was the fifteenth of the month of Lewis [Ab];" Therefore, the rebellion was on the fourteenth of Lewis (Roman), and Ab (Hebrew). (August, 66 A.D.[16:Date 1])

The massacre of tens of thousands of Jews and the choosing of generals
Book II Ch. XVIII

Shortly after that the Caesareans killed the Jews living in Caesarea, which Jews were innocent of doing anything wrong. "Insomuch that in one hour's time above 20,000 Jews were killed, and all Caesarea was emptied of its Jewish inhabitants; for Florus caught such as ran away, and sent them in bonds to the galleys."[16:15]

That enraged the Jews and several parties attacked and set on fire neighboring cities, Philadelphia, Sebonitis, Gerasa, and Pell. "However, the Syrians were even with the Jews in the multitude of the men whom thy slew; for they killed those whom they caught in their cities."[16:16]

A group of Jews came to Scythopolis, were "they found Jews that acted as enemies."[16:17] They preferring safety rather than fighting were told to wait in a nearby grove. Then during the third night the people of Scythopolis slew them. "The number that was slain was above 13,000."[16:18]

"Only the Antiochians, the Sidonians, and Apamians spared those that dwelt with them, and they would not endure either to kill any of the Jews or to put them in bonds."[16:19]

The Bible speaks of Antioch as a place where Paul, Peter, and Silas had been and where they were first called Christians 'little Christs' by the Greeks.

Cestius marched from Ptolemais and came to Caesarea; he then sent part of his army [Romans] for a surprise attack on Joppa. "The number of the slain was 8400."[16:20]

Book II Ch, XIX

"But when Cestius had marched from Antipatris to Lydda, he found the city empty of its men, for the whole multitude were gone up to Jerusalem to the Feast of Tabernacles; yet did he destroy fifty of those that showed themselves, and burnt the city."[16:21] After that, he marched forward and camped near Jerusalem. Even though it was a Sabbath day the Jews fell upon the Romans and killed 515, but when the front of the Jewish army became cut off; they returned to the city. In Jerusalem Agrippa tried to persuade that Cestius would give them his right hand and forgive them if they would lay down their arms; however, the seditious [rebels] killed the ambassadors and that upset the people. Cestius, observing the disturbances among the Jews moved his camp within seven furlongs of the city. Then after four days he brought his army into the city. The seditious became frightened and retreated to the inner city and the Temple. Cestius set the Cenopolis [new city] and timber-market on fire. "After which he came to the upper city, and pitched his camp over against the royal palace."[16:22] Seized by fear many of the seditious ran out of the city. The soldiers "got all things ready for setting fire to the gate of the Temple,"[16:23] and they could have taken the city if they had continued a little longer.

However, Josephus writes, "But it was, I suppose, owing to the aversion God had already at the city and sanctuary, that he was hindered from putting an end to the war that very day."[16:24] "By despairing of any expectation of taking it, without having received any disgrace, he [Cestius] retired from the city."[16:25] As the Romans retreated, the rebels kept attacking them from the rear and the Romans left much of their equipment behind. It was a disaster for the Romans.

Book II Ch. XX

When the people of Damascus were informed of the defeat of the Romans, they sought to kill the Jews that were cooped up in the gymnasium without their wives knowing, since many of them favored Judaism, "So they came upon the Jews, and cut their throats, as being in a narrow place, in number 10,000."[16:26]

Josephus was put in charge of the defense of both Galilees

After those who pursued Cestius returned to Jerusalem, they decided that they needed to choose leaders.

"Josephus, the son of Matthias, of both the Galilees. Gamala also, which was the strongest city in those parts, was put under his command."[16:27]

Josephus sought the trust of those cities in Galilee and at first it went well. He fortified cities and had walls built in proper places. "He also got together more than 100.000 young men, all of whom he armed with the old weapons which he had collected together and prepared for them."[16:28]

Book II Ch. XXI

John son of Levi, a native of Gischala, schemed to replace Josephus as leader by saying that "Josephus was delivering up the administration of affairs to the Romans; and many such plots did he lay in order to ruin him."[16:29]

John caused towns to be stirred up. "Some he corrupted with delusive frauds, and others with money, and so persuaded them to revolt from Josephus.[16:30]

Josephus sought to put down rebellion without killing.

Josephus made a public proclamation that he would burn the houses down of those that did not forsake John in five days. "Whereupon 3000 of John's party left him immediately."[16:31] "John then took himself, together with his 2000 Syrian renegades, from open attempts, to more secret ways of treachery."[16:32]

Book II Ch. XXII

Simon son of Gioras got a band together and they ravaged the country. "And when the army was sent against him by Ananus, and the other rulers. He and his band retired to the robbers that were at Masada, and stayed there, and plundered the country of Idumea with them, till Ananus and his other adversaries were slain."[16:33]

Book III Ch I-VII

Nero gave Flavius Vespasian command of the armies in Syria to put down the Jewish rebellion. Vespasian proceeded from Antioch of Syria joined by King Agrippa with his forces and was later joined by Titus son of Vespasian with a legion from Alexandria, Egypt. The Roman legions slew many men along the way and as they arrived near Jotapata in Galilee, Josephus hurried there from Tiberias to lead their defense. The Jews in Jotapata repelled the Romans for forty-seven days until the Romans got over a wall. The Romans butchered the men, "Excepting the infants and the women and of these there were gathered together as captives 1200; and as for those that were slain, at the taking of the city, and in the former fights, they were numbered to be 40,000. So Vespasian gave order that the city should be demolished, and all the fortifications burnt down."[16:34]

The Capture of Josephus
Bk III Ch VIII

During the massacre as the Romans were upon them, Josephus, "leaped into a certain deep pit, whereto there adjoined a large den at one side of it, which den could not be seen by those that were above ground."[16:35]

There were 40 other persons hiding in the den with Josephus. On the third day, they were discovered and Vespasian sent two tribunes to offer Josephus their right hand, but Josephus refused to surrender. Vespasian sent Nicanor, a tribune friend of Josephus, assuring him he would be saved because of his valor. He hesitated at first then, "Josephus called to mind the dreams which he had dreamed in the nighttime, whereby God had signified to him beforehand both the future calamities of the Jews, and the events that concerned the Roman emperors."[16:36]

Josephus silently prayed to God and said, "Since thou hast made choice of this soul of mine to foretell what is to come to pass hereafter, I willingly give them my hands, and am content to live. And I protest openly, that I do not go over to the Romans as a deserter of the Jews, but as a minister from thee."[16:37]

The other persons in the cavern threatened to kill Josephus if he submitted to the Romans. Josephus convinced them it was better to die by each other's hand than by one's own and that it should be determined by drawing lots.

"He whom the lot falls on first, let him be killed by him that hath the second lot, and thus fortune shall make its progress through us all; nor shall any of us perish by his own right hand."[16:38] After it got down to Josephus and one other man, he convinced him they should surrender.

Vespasian intending to bring Josephus to Nero, Josephus said, "Dost thou send me to Nero? For why? Are Nero's successors till they come to thee still alive? Thou, O Vespasian, art Caesar and emperor, thou and this thy son."[16:39]

The Death of Nero
Book IV Ch IX

"Now as Vespasian was returning to Caesarea, and was getting ready with all his army to march directly to Jerusalem, he was informed that Nero was dead, after he had reigned thirteen years and eight days."[16:40]

After Vespasian heard the news that Nero was dead, he decided to cease the attack on Jerusalem and wait for instructions. "When he [Vespasian] heard that Galba was made emperor, he attempted nothing till he also should send him some directions about the war: however, he [Vespasian] sent his son Titus, to salute him, and receive his command about the Jews."[16:41]

Titus and King Agrippa set sail to Rome, but along the way "they heard that Galba was slain;"[16:42] therefore, Titus returned to

Caesarea. Ortho had taken over managing the government as emperor. The legions of Germany declared Vitellius emperor; they defeated the forces of Ortho and Ortho committed suicide.

Book IV CH. X

Upon hearing that Vitellius's troops had plundered Roman citizens, Vespasian's troops declared Vespasian emperor. Since Egypt supplied the grain for Rome, Vespasian sent a letter to "Tiberius Alexander, who was then governor of Egypt and of Alexandria."[16:43] While Vespasian's troops were en route, Tiberius Alexander took an oath to Vespasian. News spread of Vespasian and in addition, the legions in Mysia and Pannonia also took oaths to Vespasian.

Josephus' chains removed

Vespasian remembered Josephus' prediction, "so he called for Josephus, and commanded that he should be set at liberty."[16:44]
Titus advised, "For if we do not barely loose his bonds, but cut them to pieces, he will be like a man that hath never been bound at all."[16:45] "For that is the usual method as to such as has been bound without cause. This advice was agreed to by Vespasian."[16:46]

Book IV Ch. XI

Vespasian sent a considerable part of his army commanded by Mucianus to go to Italy. They were joined by a third of the army from Mysia commanded by Antonius Primus. Together they overcame the forces of Vitellius.

Vespasian was in Alexandria when he heard the news that he had been declared emperor. He went to Rome, "but sent his son Titus, with a select part of his army to destroy Jerusalem"[16:47]
so Titus marched from Egypt to Caesarea.

Book V Ch. I

The rebels had fled to Jerusalem. John of Gischala led a large group of Zealots. Eleazar could not stand to submit to John, who was younger than himself and withdrew with a group taking control of the inner court of the Temple. Simon, son of Giora, led another group that had control of the upper city and a large part of the lower. They fought among themselves and burned each other's corn supply and other provisions. During the pause in the attack people had come to Jerusalem from the country for the Jews had begun celebrating the Feast of Unleavened Bread.

Book V Ch III

"On the Feast of Unleavened Bread, which was now come, it being the fourteenth day of the month."[16:48] "Eleazar and his party opened the gates of this [innermost court of the] Temple, and admitted such of the people as were desirous to worship God into it."[16:49] John and his party entered with concealed weapons and attacked and scattered Eleazar's party.

The 70 AD Roman attack on Jerusalem led by Titus
Book V Ch IV

"The city of Jerusalem was fortified with three walls, on such parts as were not encompassed with impossible valleys; for in such places it had but one wall."[16:50]

The Roman army consisting of several legions led by Titus breached the first wall with catapults. The Jews retreated behind the second wall.

Book V Ch VIII

After five days the Romans made a narrow passage in the second wall. A thousand-armed Romans entered through the breach. The Jews fought the Romans in the narrow streets and the Romans made a difficult retreat.

"And thus were the Romans driven out, after they had possessed themselves of the second wall."[16:51] Titus ordered that the second wall should be demolished entirely.

Book V Ch. IX

Titus decided to relax the siege for a while. Commanders put the legions into full battle-array as they were being paid, a ceremony that lasted four days.

Titus, "sent Josephus to speak to them [the Jews] in their own language; for he imagined they might yield to the persuasion of a countryman of their own."[16:52]

From a place outside of the wall, Josephus spoke at length about the might of the Romans and the history of the Jews. When the king of Egypt, seized Sarah, who was Abrahams wife, God defended her from his advances. "When Sennacherib, king of Syria, brought along with him all Asia, and encompassed this city round with his army, did he fall by the hands of men? Were not those hands lifted up to god in prayers, without meddling with their arms, when an angel of God destroyed that prodigious army in one night? When the Assyrian king, as he rose next day, found 185,000 dead bodies, and when he, with the remainder of his army, fled away from the Hebrews, though they were unarmed, and did not pursue them!"[16:53]

"And, to speak in general, we can produce no example wherein our fathers got any success by war, or failed of success when without war they committed themselves to God."[16:54] "Wherefore, I cannot but suppose that God is fled out of his sanctuary, and stands on the side of those against whom you fight." [16:55]

Josephus advised them to lay down their arms and save the city, the Temple and take pity on their families, "who will be gradually consumed either by famine or by war. I am sensible that this danger will extend to my mother and wife."[16:56]

<table><tr><td>

It's not that God stood on the side of the Romans; It's that the glory of the Lord had left the Temple because of the sufficiency of the atoning sacrificial death of the Messiah, the Ruler, Jesus on the cross. The people of the ruler to come, [the antichrist], took advantage and destroyed the Temple.

</td></tr></table>

Book V Ch. X

The seditious [rebels] did not yield to what Josephus told them. On the fifth day, Titus ordered the army to begin building two ramps to the third wall. Apparently, the ramps were made of wood since later on in the battle, they had to go a great distance to find wood for building ramps.

Some of the people swallowed pieces of gold and escaped to the Romans and Titus let them go into the country. "John and Simon, with their factions, did more carefully watch these men's going out than they did the coming in of the Romans and, if anyone but afford the least shadow of suspicion of such an intention, his throat was cut immediately."[16:57] While, many people in Jerusalem were dying of starvation.

Book V Ch. XI

Some of the rebels and poor people went out to find food for themselves and their family intending to return with it. Those that were captured by the Romans "were first whipped, and then tormented with all sorts of tortures before they died, and were then crucified before the wall of the city."[16:58] This amounted to 500 or more per day. Titus did not forbid it in the hope that "the Jews might, perhaps, yield at that sight."[16:59]
Yet, the Jews managed to set the Romans' machines on fire.

Book V Ch. XII

Titus decided to build a wall around the whole city and the Romans completed a wall that encompassed the city.
"Then did the famine widen its progress, and devoured the people by whole houses and families."[16:60] "The lanes of the city were full of dead bodies of the aged; the children also and the young men wandered about the marketplaces like shadows, all swelled with the famine, and fell down dead wheresoever their misery seized them."[16:61]
Titus ordered banks to be built again. They traveled a distance of ninety furlongs to find more wood and managed to rise banks in four parts.

Book V Ch. XIII

Matthias the son of Boethus, and one of the high priests had persuaded the people to admit Simon into the city; Yet, Simon "condemned *him* to die for being on the side of the Romans."[16:62]
The rebels put Josephus's father in prison and made a proclamation prohibiting anyone from speaking to him.
After a certain Syrian deserter "was caught gathering pieces of gold out of the excrement of the Jews bellies,"[16:63] the fame of it spread, "So the multitude of the Arabians, with the Syrians, cut up those that came as supplicants, and searched their bellies."[16:64] "In one nights time about 2000 of these deserters were thus dissected."[16:65]

In Jerusalem carcasses lay in heaps, "as those were to go in battle array who had been already used to 10,000 murders, and must tread upon those dead bodies as they marched along."[16:66] "But as they had their right hands already polluted with the murders of their own countrymen, and in that condition ran out to fight with foreigners, they seemed to me [Josephus] to have cast a reproach upon God himself, as if he were too slow in punishing them."[16:67]

The Romans were battering the tower of Antonia and had removed four stones from it; yet, it stood in place, but during the night the wall next to it suddenly fell down. "The unexpected joy of the Romans, at this fall of the wall, soon quenched by the sight they had of another wall, which John and his party had built within it."[16:68]

It would be hazardous for the Romans to scale John's wall because the rebels could throw darts down on them from the tower of Antonia, so Titus gave a long speech about the virtue of dying in battle.

After Titus finished his speech, Sabinus, a Syrian, covered himself with his shield and proceeded to the wall. Eleven men followed him. Sabinus managed to get to the top of the wall and not knowing how many Romans there were the Jews fled. Inside the wall Sabinus tripped on a large stone and fell with a loud noise. The Jews turned and noticed he was alone. Covered over with darts Sabinus died. Three of the men outside of the wall were killed; eight others were wounded and carried back to camp.

Two days later during the night, twelve men that were on the forefront got together with "the standard-bearer of the fifth legion,"[16:69] two horsemen, and a trumpeter. Without making noise, they went to the tower of Antonia. "When they had cut the throats of the first guards of the place, as they were asleep, they got possession of the wall, and ordered the trumpeter to sound his trumpet."[16:70]

Imagining there were many Romans, the other guards ran away. Upon hearing the signal, Caesar ordered the army to put on their armor and came there with his commanders "and first of all ascended [the wall], as did the chosen men that were with him."[16:71] The Jews retreated and those of John and those of Simon fought the Romans from taking the Temple area. They fought in close hand to hand "from the ninth hour of the night until the seventh hour of the day."[16:72] The Jews came in crowds and the Romans had only part of their army, "so it was at present thought sufficient by the Romans to take possession of the tower of Antonia."[16:73]

Book VI Ch. II

Titus gave orders to dig up the foundation of the tower of Antonia to make a ready passage for his army. Titus had been informed that "on that very day, which was the seventeenth day of Panemus [Tamuz], the sacrifice called 'the Daily Sacrifice' had failed and had not been offered to God for want of men to offer it, and that the people were grievously troubled at it."[16:74] Titus sent Josephus to call to John in the Hebrew language to come out with his men and fight "without the danger of destroying either his city or temple."[16:75]

"In the meantime, the rest of the Roman army had in seven days' time, overthrown [some] foundations of the tower of Antonia, and had made a ready and broad way to the temple. Then did the legions come near the first court*, and began to raise their banks."[16:76]
* The court of the Gentiles

The Jerusalem temple destroyed
Book VI Ch. IV

The Roman "engines had battered the wall [of the inner temple] for six days without ceasing, without making any impression on it."[16:77] Other Romans had removed a stone from under the Northern Gate, yet the gate stood. The Romans brought ladders to the cloisters, but when they came to the top, the Jews threw them backward.

"But when Titus perceived that his endeavors to spare a foreign temple turned to the damage of his soldiers, and made them be killed, he gave orders to set the gates on fire."[16:78] "The silver that was over them quickly carried the flames to the wood that was within it, whence it spread itself all on the sudden, and caught hold of the cloisters."[16:79]

Josephus speaks of the stone wall around the Temple on the Temple Mount, see pictures on pages 84 and 85.

The stone wall took the place of the linen curtain of the Tabernacle in the Wilderness. From the outside there was only one entrance on only one side of the linen curtain into the court area. When entering the court, the first furnishing was the Brazen Altar where sacrifices for sin were made. There was a ramp leading to the top of the Brazen Altar.

Such a wall would explain Jesus saying in John 10:1 **"Most assuredly, I say to you, he who does not enter by the door, but climbs up some other way, the same is a thief and a robber."** and John 10:9 **"I am the door. If anyone enters by me, he will be saved, and will go in and out and find pasture."**

Although, Josephus speaks of more than one gate in the stone wall around the Temple on the Temple Mount in Jerusalem; also, there wasn't a court of the Gentiles in the Tabernacle in the Wilderness beyond which Gentiles could not go as there was in the Temple.

According to Josephus, the gates of the wall were covered with silver and the silver conducted the heat of the fire making the wood burn faster until it spread to the cloisters [or porticoes], the buildings around the edge of the Temple Mount, which were partly burned by fire at that time. In the Tabernacle in the Wilderness, gold represented divinity, silver represented salvation, bronze or copper represented judgement, and acacia wood represented humanity.

"But then, the next day, Titus commanded part of his army to quench the fire."[16:80]

Titus gathered his commanders together to give their advice about what should be done with the holy house. Titus decided that they should not take revenge on things that are inanimate. They retired for the night planning to attack in the morning.

"But as for that house, God had for certain long ago doomed it to the fire; and now that fatal day was come according to the revolution of ages: it was the tenth day of the month Lous [Ab], upon which it was formerly burnt by the king of Babylon."[16:81]

Some of the Romans were quenching fires that burned in the inner court near the Temple. One soldier without orders snatched some material out of the fire "and being lifted up by another soldier, he set fire to a golden window, through which there was a passage to the rooms that were round about the holy house, on the north side of it."[16:82]

Titus, his commanders, and several legions came running to the fire. The Romans slew the seditious [rebels] weak with hunger. "Now round about the altar lay dead bodies heaped one upon another; as at the steps going up to it ran a great quantity of their blood."[16:83]

The flames had not yet reached the inner part of the temple and Titus thought it might yet be saved. Rather the soldiers' passions were "their hatred of the Jews,"[16:84] and "moreover, the hope of plunder induced many to go on, as having the opinion that all the places within were full of money, and seeing that all round about it, was made of gold."[16:85]

Herod's Temple was destroyed by the Romans in the same month and on the same day of the month as Solomon's Temple was destroyed by Nebuchadnezzar's army

"For the same month and day were now observed, as I said before, wherein the holy house was burnt formerly by the Babylonians. Now, the number of years that passed from its first foundation, which was laid by King Solomon, till this its destruction, which happened in the second year of the reign of Vespasian are collected to be 1130, besides seven months and fifteen days."[16:86]

The Temple was doomed the tenth day of the month of Lous (Roman) (Ab 10 Hebrew) (August 6, 70 A.D. Julian). Jeremiah 52:12 gives the date, **"The fifth month on the tenth day of the month,"** for the burning of the house of the Lord in the nineteenth year of King Nebuchadnezzar. The Jews date it as the day after the Sabbath, Ab 9 (8/5 Julian) and during the priestly course Jehoiarib; furthermore, Jewish tradition dates the destruction of both Temples as Ab 9.

Book VI Ch.VI

Then Titus spoke saying, "Henceforth treat them according to the laws of war. So he gave orders to the soldiers both to burn and to plunder the city; who did nothing indeed, that day, but on the next day they set fire to the repository of the archives, to Acra, to the council-house, and to the place called Ophlas; at which time the fire proceeded as far as the palace of Queen Helena, which was in the middle of Acra."[16:87]

Book VI Ch. VIII

Two candlesticks were saved from the Temple fire and plunder because they were hidden in the Temple Wall.

After receiving an oath of security from Caesar, a priest "delivered him from the wall of the holy house two candlesticks like those that lay in the holy house, with tables and cisterns and veils, all made of solid gold, and very heavy. He also delivered to him the veils and the garments, with the precious stones."[16:88]

After the treasurer of the Temple "was seized on, and showed Titus the coats and girdles of the priests, with a great quantity of purple and scarlet, which were there reposited for the uses of the veil"[16:89] along with spices and sacred ornaments delivered to Titus obtained his pardon.

The Romans took the upper city where Simon had been in control and Titus set Fronto in control of the fate of the captives.

Book VI Ch. IX

Titus set his friend Fronto in charge of determining the fate of the captives. He "slew all those that had been seditious and robbers."[16:90] The tallest and most beautiful were reserved to the triumph celebration, the rest of those over 17 were sent to work in Egyptian mines and those under 17 were sold as slaves. "Now, during the days wherein Fronto was distinguishing these men, there perished, for want of food 11,000."[16:91]

"Now the number of those that were carried captive during this whole war was collected to be 97,000; as was the number of those that perished during the whole siege 1,100,000."[16:92] Many of them were from the countryside, who had come to celebrate the Feast of Unleavened Bread.

John surrendered; Simon hid for a while

The Romans searched for those that hid underground and slew 2000. John surrendered and begged the Romans to give him their right hand for his security, a thing that he did not do for others. He was eventually sent to prison.

Book VI Ch. X

"And thus was Jerusalem taken, in the second year of the reign of Vespasian, on the eighth day of the month Gorpieus [Elul]."[16:93]

Book VII Ch. I

"Caesar gave orders that they should now demolish the entire city and the temple, but should leave as many of the towers standing as were of the greatest eminence; that is, Phasaelus, Hippicus, and Mariamne, and so much of the wall as enclosed the city on the west side."[16:94] "The towers also spared, in order to demonstrate to posterity what kind of city it was, and how well fortified, which the Roman valor had subdued."[16:95]

Then the list was read of those "that had performed great exploits in this war."[16:96]

Titus called to them as they were read; they were given gold crowns and spears of gold, and besides this he distributed the gold and silver spoils of war among them.

Book VII Ch. II

Titus marched from Caesarea to Caesarea Philippi and exhibited shows there. "A great number of the captives were destroyed; some being thrown to wild beasts, and others, in multitudes, forced to kill one another, as if they were enemies. And here it was that Titus was informed of the seizure of Simon."[16:97]

Simon had been in the upper city, but when the Roman army had gotten within the walls, then together with a group of his men, which included stonecutters, went into the subterraneous cavern. They dug beyond the old digging in hopes of coming out at a safe place. When their provisions ran out, "Simon, thinking he might be able to astonish and delude the Romans, put on a white frock and buttoned upon him a purple cloak, and appeared out of the ground in the place where the Temple had formerly been."[16:98]

At first Simon would not tell the Romans near him who he was, but asked them to call their captain. Terentius Rufus, who was the commander, learned he was Simon and had him put in bonds, then he was brought to Caesarea when Titus returned there again.

Book VII Ch. V

Titus departed for Egypt and then by sea to Italy. He brought with him Simon and John, along with 700 tall and handsome captives.

In Rome there was an elaborate parade and Simon was killed

In Rome, there was an elaborate parade with floats three or four stories high representing conquered cities.

From Jerusalem, a golden table, a golden lampstand and the Law of the Jews. After which Vespasian rode in front followed by Titus and his brother Domitian followed him.

"Now the last part of this pompous show was at the temple of Jupiter Capitolinus, whither when they come, they stood still; for it was the Romans' ancient custom to stay till somebody brought the news that the general of the enemy was slain. This general was Simon the son of Giosas, who had then been led in this triumph among the captives; a rope had also been put upon his head, and he had been drawn into a proper place in the forum, and had withal been tormented by those that drew him along; and the law of the Romans required that malefactors condemned to die should be slain there."[16:99]

Some of the articles of the Temple were saved for a while

Vespasian built a Temple to Peace; "he also laid up therein as ensigns of his glory, those golden vessels and instruments that were taken out of the Jewish Temple. But still he gave orders that they should lay up their law, and the purple veils of the holy place, in the royal palace itself, and keep them there."[16:100]

The Works of Flavius Josephus; A History Of The Jewish Wars translated by William Whiston; (The S. S. Scranton Co. Hartford, Conn. 1913)

16:1-9. Ibid., p. 848
16:10-11. Ibid., p. 702
16:12. Ibid., p. 711
16:13-14. Ibid., p. 713
16:15-17. Ibid., p. 715
16:18-19. Ibid., p. 716
16:20. Ibid., p. 718
16:21. Ibid., p. 719
16:22-25. Ibid., p. 720
16:26-27. Ibid., p. 722
16:28. Ibid., p. 723
16:29. Ibid., p. 724
16:30-32. Ibid., p.726
16:33. Ibid., p. 728
16:34-35. Ibid., p. 747
16:36-37. Ibid., p. 748
16:38-39 Ibid., p. 750

16:40-42. Ibid., p. 786
16:43. Ibid. p.792
16:44-46. Ibid., p. 793
16:47. Ibid., p 794
16:48-49 Ibid., p. 801
16:50. Ibid., p. 803
16:51. Ibid., p. 815
16:52. Ibid., p. 817
16:53-54. Ibid., p. 818
16:55-56, Ibid., p. 820
16:57. Ibid., p. 821
16:58-59. Ibid., p. 822
16:60-61 Ibid., p. 826
16:62. Ibid., p. 827
16:63-65. Ibid., p. 829
16:66-67. Ibid., p. 830
16:68. Ibid., p. 832
16:69-71. Ibid., p. 834

16:72-73. Ibid., p. 835
16:74-75. Ibid., p. 836
16:76. Ibid., p. 839
16:77. Ibid., p. 843 & 844
16:78-80. Ibid., p. 844
16:81-82. Ibid., p. 845
16:83-86. Ibid., p. 846
16:87. Ibid., p. 851
16:88-89. Ibid., p. 853
16:90-92. Ibid., p. 855
16:93. Ibid., p. 856
16:94-95. Ibid., p. 857
16:96-98. Ibid., p. 858
16:99-100. Ibid., p. 865

16:Date 1. Paul L. Maier *Josephus The Essential Works* (Kregel Publications; Grand Rapids, MI. 1988) p. 293
16:Date 2. Ibid., p. 371

Chapter 17
The Desolation of Judea
Daniel 9:26
Desolations have been decreed

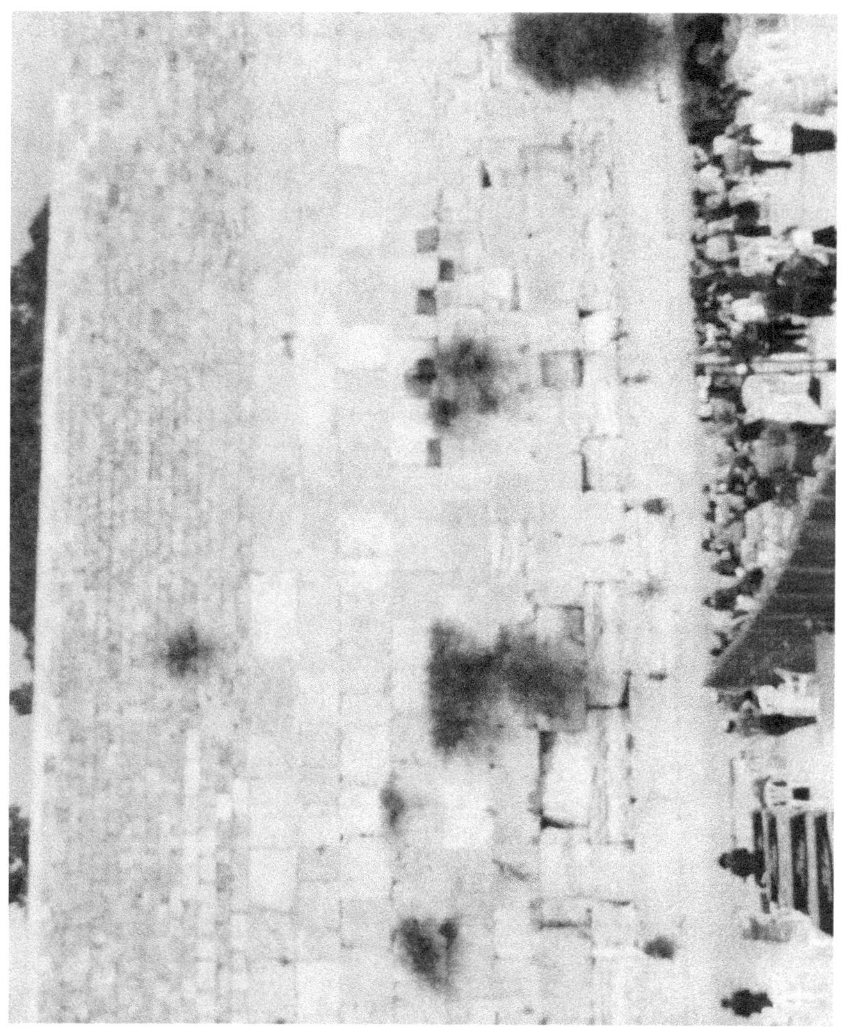

The massive Temple Mount Western Wall built by King Herod that expanded the Temple Mount further west beyond where Solomon had built it. The Western Wall of the Temple Mount was not a part of the Temple Wall, which was on top of the Temple Mount.

The present ground level is higher than it was in the first century A.D. The massive Western Wall goes down 70 feet lower than the present ground level to bedrock. Herod Agrippa I expanded the mount walls to the south beyond the Hasmonean extension and to the north and west beyond Solomon's Mount walls. The present Western Wall was not a part of the Temple. The Temple on the mount was destroyed by the Romans fulfilling the prophecies of Daniel and Jesus. Hadrian built a Temple to Jupiter on the Temple Mount. Following that the removal of stones from the Temple Mount continued during the time of the desolation of Judea. Eusebius speaks of people taking stones from the Temple [Hadrian's] for their own use, and apparently Justinian used stones from the Temple Mount to help build on the Church of Our Lady.

Jerusalem was left desolate in 70 A.D.

Book VI Ch. X

Josephus writes, "And thus Jerusalem was taken in the second year of the reign of Vespasian, on the eighth day of the month Gorpiaeus [Elul]."[17:1] (September 26, A.D. 70[17:Date 1])

Book VII Ch. I

"Caesar gave orders that they should now demolish the entire city and the Temple, but should leave as many of the towers standing as were of the greatest eminence; that is, Phasaelus, Hippicus, and Mariamne, and so much of the wall as enclosed the city on the west side."[17:2] "The towers also spared, in order to demonstrate to posterity what kind of city it was, and how well fortified, which the Roman valor had subdued."[17:3]

Masada was left desolate in 73 A.D.

After the desolation of Jerusalem, there was the desolation of the fortress of Masada.

Book VII Ch. VIII

"Upon this top of the hill, Jonathan the high priest first of all built a fortress and called it Masada.[17:4]

King Herod rebuilt the residence

"he also built a wall round about the entire top of the hill."[16:5] "There were also erected upon that wall thirty-eight towers, each of them fifty cubits high." [17:6]

The *sicarii* had taken control of Masada. It had a narrow steep path to get to the top. Over a long period of time, the Romans built a ramp of earthworks to assist the army getting to the top.

Eleazar the leader of the *sicarii* convinced those with him that the Romans would eventually overcome them and that it would be nobler to die by their own hands than to fall into the hands of the Romans.

Book VII Ch. IX

The men while weeping killed their own familes. Then those men drew lots. Ten men killed the remaining men while they lay next to their familes. The ten remaining men drew lots again. The last man set a fire and then he killed himself.

"Yet was there an ancient woman, and another who was kin to Eleazar … with five children, who had concealed themselves in caverns underground."[17:7] "Those others were 960 in number."[17:8] "This calamitous slaughter was made on the fifteenth day of the month Xanthicus [Nisan]."[17:9] (May 2, A.D. 73[17:Date 2]).

When the women heard the noise of the Romans coming, they went out and told the Romans what had been done and that they had attempted to put the fire out.

Masada was left desolate.

The Roman Emperor Hadrian built a Temple to the Roman god Jupiter on the Jerusalem Temple Mount

In 131 A.D. the Roman Emperor Hadrian ordered that Jerusalem should be replaced by a Roman city with a Temple to the Roman god Jupiter on the destroyed Temple site.

"In Jerusalem he founded a city in the place of the one which had been razed to the ground, naming it Aelia Capitolina, and on the site of the Temple Mount of the god he raised a new Temple to Jupiter. This brought on a war of no slight importance nor of brief duration, for the Jews deemed it intolerable that foreign races should be settled in their city and foreign religious rites planted there."

Dio Cassius, *Roman History,* Book LXIX, 12. 1 & 2.[17:10]

In 132 A.D. Hadrian forbid castration and circumcision.

Judaea was left desolate by 135 A.D.

The Bar Kokhba revolt against Hadrian (132-135 A.D.) led by Simon ben Kosevah resulted in the desolation of much of Judaea.

Simon ben Kosevah led a revolt that annihilated the local Roman legion, and he established an independent Jewish state that lasted three years with himself as Nasi 'prince.' Rabbi Akiva proclaimed ben Kosevah as Bar Kokhba 'son of the star' in fulfillment of Balaam's prophecy in Numbers 24:17, **"A star shall come out of Jacob."** Simon thought of himself as the Messiah.

Justin Martyr (100 - 165 A.D.) referred to Simon ben Kosevah by his implied messianic name Bar-Cochba as he wrote:

"For in the Jewish war which lately happened Bar-Cochba, the leader of the revolt of the Jews, gave orders that Christians alone should be led to terrible punishments, unless they would deny Jesus the Christ and blaspheme,"

Justin Martyr, *First Apology* 31.[17:11]

The Roman army returned and fought a scorched earth battle for two-and-a-half years until Simon ben Kosevah was killed and his forces were defeated by 135 A.D.

"Very few Jews in fact survived. Fifty of their most important outposts and nine hundred and eighty-five of their most famous villages were razed to the ground. Five hundred and eighty thousand men were slain in the various raids and battles, and the number of those that perished by famine, disease or fire was past finding out. Thus nearly the whole of Judaea was made desolate, a result of which the people had had forewarning before the war."

Dio Cassius, *Roman history*, Book LXIX 14. 1 & 2.[17:12]

In addition, Hadrian built a Temple to Venus supposedly over the Tomb of Jesus. Hadrian barred those who were circumcised from entering the city of Aelia under penalty of death.

The war took a toll on the Romans, too. When the legions returned to Rome, they did not do their usual celebrating. It was a tragedy for both sides. The Province of Judaea along with Galilee and Samaria were formed into a new province named Syria Palaestina. It was the end of a Jewish state until 1948.

Eusebius Pamphilus of Caesarea (260-339 A.D.), an early Christian Church historian, tells of people taking stones from the Temple Mount and using them for personal and pagan purposes.

"So Aquila says, 'Therefore for your sake the land of Zion shall be ploughed, and Jerusalem shall be a quarry of stone,' for being inhabited by men of foreign race it is even now like a quarry, all the inhabitants of the city choosing stores from its ruins as they will for private as well as public buildings. And it is sad for the eyes to see stones from the Temple itself, and from its ancient sanctuary and holy place, used for the building of idol temples, and of theatres for the populace."

The Proof of the Gospel, being Eusebius, Demonstratio Evangelica, (314-318 A.D.), Vol. II, Book VIII. 3 (406) (d).[17:13]

Aquila of Sinope wrote a Greek translation of the Hebrew Old Testament around 140 A.D. It only exists in some fragments and quotations today. Eusebius quotes Micah 3:12 as being fulfilled before his eyes. The stones that were being removed from the Temple Mount during the time of Eusebius would have been from Hadrian's Temple to Jupiter.

The Emperor Constantine

Eusebius Pamphilus *The Life of The Blessed Emperor Constantine*

In Book 3 Ch. VI, Eusebius the Church historian who was alive at that time speaks of Constantine ordering a council to assemble at Nicaea.[17:14] In Ch XXV, Eusebius speaks of Constantine ordering a house of prayer be built in the "locality of our Savior's resurrection an object of attraction and veneration to all."[17:15] In Ch. XXVI, Eusebius describes that the tomb had been covered by a massive mound and paved with stone.[17:16] In Ch. XXVII, the Temple of Venus over the Tomb of Jesus was cast down and Constantine "gave further orders that the materials of what was thus destroyed, both stone and timber, should be removed and thrown as far from the spot as possible."[17:17] In Ch. XXVII, Constantine "directed that the ground itself should be dug up to a considerable depth, and the soil which had been polluted by the foul impurities of demon worship transported to a far distant place.[17:18] In Ch. XXVIII, "As soon as the original surface of the ground, beneath the covering of earth, appeared, immediately, and contrary to all expectations, the venerable and hallowed monument of our Savior's resurrection was discovered.[17:19] In Ch. XXIX, "Immediately after the transactions I have recorded, the Emperor sent forth injunctions which breathed a truly pious spirit, at the same time granting ample supplies of money, and commanding that a house of prayer worthy of the worship of God should be erected near the Savior's Tomb on a scale of rich and royal greatness."[17:20] In Ch. XXIX, "He lad his commands, therefore, on the Governors of the Eastern Provinces, that by an abundant and unsparing expenditure they should secure the completion of the work on a scale of noble and ample magnificence."[17:21]

In Ch. XXIX, Constantine wrote to Macarius, Bishop of the Church at Jerusalem saying, "It will be well, therefore, for your Sagacity to make such arrangements and provisions of all things needful for the work"[17:22] In Ch. XXXI, "And as to the columns and marbles, whatever you shall judge, after actual inspection of the plan, to be especially precious and serviceable, be diligent to send information to us in writing, in order that whatever materials and in whatever quality we shall esteem from your letter to be needful, may be procured from every quarter, as required."[17:23]

In Ch. XLIII, Helena Augusta, Constantine's mother ordered two churches to be built. One at Bethlehem, "the scene of the Savior's birth; the other on the mount of his ascension," the Mount of Olives.[17:24]

In Book 4 Ch. XLVII, Eusebius speaks of the Council at Nicaea being held in the twentieth year and the dedication of the Church at the Sepulcher of our Savior in the thirtieth anniversary of the reign of Constantine.[17:25] In Ch. XXXVI, Eusebius speaks of Constantine instructing him "to order fifty copies of the sacred scriptures."[17:26]

In Ch. LIV, in several cities heathen temples were stripped of their doors at his command. "Having formed this resolution, he considered no military force needful of this repression of evil: a few of his own friends sufficed for this service," They ordered the priests themselves to bring their gods to the light of day, then the idols were melted down in fire.[17:27]

Eusebius Pamphilus, *The Life of The Blessed Emperor Constantine*. It was completed between the death of Constantine in 337 A.D. and before the death of Eusebius in 339 A.D.

Apparently, the Temple of Venus built by Hadrian, supposedly, over the Tomb of Jesus was an attempt to disrespect Christians. Then several years later, Constantine ordered it torn down and the Church at the Sepulcher of Our Savior be built there.

Eusebius does not specifically mention that Constantine had the Temple of Jupiter on the Temple Mount destroyed; it may be that it was destroyed by people removing stones for their own use.

The Emperor Julian (nicknamed the apostate) reigned 361-363 A.D.

Another example that speaks of the sufficiency of the atoning sacrificial death of Jesus on the cross happened during the reign of Emperor Julian. He was a Roman Emperor after Constantine, but he was not a Christian. Ammianus Marcellinus writes of his friend Julianus Augustus's failed attempt to rebuild a Jerusalem Temple.

"2. And although he weighed every possible variety of events with anxious thought, and pushed on with burning zeal the many preparations for his campaign, yet turning his activity to every part, and eager to extend the memory of his reign by great works, he planned at vast cost to restore the once splendid Temple at Jerusalem, which after many mortal combats during the siege by Vespasian and later by Titus, had barely been stormed. He had entrusted the speedy performance of this work to Alypius of Antioch, who had once been vice-prefect of Britain. 3. But, though this Alypius pushed the works on with vigor, aided by the governor of the province, terrifying balls of flame kept bursting forth near the foundations of the Temple, and made the place inaccessible to the workmen, some of whom were burned to death; and since in this way the elements persistently resisted them. Julian gave up the attempt."[17:28]
Ammianus Marcellinus, Book XXIII. 1, 2-3

Apparently, the earthquake in Galilee in 363 A.D. caused underground natural gas below the surface to seep out around the foundation. As workmen would cause a spark the gas would explode and scorch them. That repeated until they gave up.

Christians at the time took it as an act of God. A Christological explanation for needing to cease the building of the Temple in 363 A.D. is that it is another testimony of the sufficiency of the atoning sacrificial death of Jesus Christ on the cross.

The Emperor Justinian

The primary source for Justinian's extensive building projects is Procopius *Buildings*. The building of the Jerusalem church is described by Procopius in *Buildings* V. vi. 1-26. The Jerusalem Church was built in the 530/40's dedicated to the Mother of God, but it was not built on the Temple Mount. Justinian ordered that the Church be built on the highest hill and he specified the length and breadth of it; however, the foundation extended beyond the hill to the east and the south. Massive pillars were brought in cut from the hills before the city and carried on specially built wagons pulled by 40 oxen. These pillars were set in the side of the hill to support the Church that extended beyond the hill.

"But when the impossibility of this task was causing the Emperor to become impatient, God revealed a natural supply of stone perfectly suited to this purpose in the near by hills, one which had either lain there in concealment previously, or was created at that moment."[17:29]
Procopius *Buildings* V. vi. 19.

It appears that Roman Emperor Hadrian's Temple to the Roman god Jupiter on the Temple Mount had been completely destroyed by the time of the Emperor Justinian and remains from Hadrian's Temple were used to build on Justinian's Jerusalem Church; thus, the Temple Mount was cleared of stones. Later, Justinian's Jerusalem Church was destroyed by the Muslims.

17:1. *The Works of Flavius Josephus; A History Of The Jewish Wars* trans. by William Whiston (Hartford, CN: The S. S. Scranton Co., 1913) p. 856

17:2-3. Ibid., p. 857; 17:4-6. Ibid., p.872; 17:7-9. Ibid., p. 878

17:10. Dio Cassius, *Roman History* Books 61-70, translated by Earnest Cary (Loeb Classical Library 176 Cambridge, MA: Harvard University Press, 1925) p. 447

17:11. Justin Martyr, *Ancient Christian Writers, St. Justin Martyr the First and Second Apologies,* trans. by Leslie William Barnard, (N. Y., NY: Paulist Press, 1997) p. 44.

17:12. Dio Cassius, *Roman History* Books 61-70, translated by Earnest Cary, Loeb Classical Library 176 (Cambridge, MA: Harvard University. Press, 1925) pp. 449 & 450.

17:13. *The proof of the Gospel,* twin brooks series, two volumes in one, being Eusebius, Demonstratio Evangelica, ed. and trans. by W. J. Ferrar, (Grand Rapids, MI: Baker Book House, 1981) P. 141

17:14. Eusebius Pamphilus, *The Life of The Blessed Emperor Constantine,* in four books: from 306 to 337 A.D. (London: Samuel Bagster and Sons, 1845) p. 119.

17:15. Ibid., p. 136; 17:16. Ibid., p. 137; 17:17. Ibid., p. 138;

17:18. Ibid., pp. 138 & 139; 17:19. Ibid., p. 139; 17:20. Ibid., p. 139.

17:21. Ibid., p. 140; 17:22. Ibid., p. 141; 17:23. Ibid., p. 142.

17:24. Ibid., p. 148; 17:25. Ibid., pp. 213 & 214; 17:26. Ibid., p. 204.

17:27. Ibid., pp. 158 & 159.

17:28. Ammianus Marcellinus, *History* II, Books 20-26 trans. by John C. Rolfe, (Loeb Classical Library 315 Cambridge, MA: Harvard University Press, 1936) P. 311

17:29. Procopius VII *Buildings.* Trans. H. B. Dewing, (Loeb Classical Library 343 Cambridge, MA: Harvard University Press, 1940 & 1954) P. 347

17:Date 1. Paul L. Maier *Josephus The Essential Works* (Kregel Publications, Grand Rapids, MI. 1988) p. 378

17:Date 2. Ibid., p. 395

Chapter 18
The built-in time gap in the seventy sevens prophecy in the counting of the sevens after the Messiah is cut off

The counting of the sevens begins with the issuing of the decree and then continues until the Messiah, the Ruler, comes. **From····the decree·····until the Messiah, the Ruler, comes there will be seven sevens and sixty-two sevens.**

The counting of the seven sevens and sixty-two sevens leads to the month of Nisan in 33 A.D. That is the month of the triumphal entry, the crucifixion, and the resurrection of Jesus from the dead.

From the issuing of the decree the counting of the sevens begins with seven sevens and sixty-two sevens, then the counting of the sevens pauses. Following that there is a parenthetical statement that refers back to the time of the first seven sevens (the years it took to rebuild the wall of Jerusalem in times of trouble and following years as there were those in the neighborhood that opposed them.)

After the pause in the counting of sevens there are two singular specific events listed and two plural general events listed.

Verse 26 makes it clear that there is a pause in the counting of the sevens when it says, **"After the sixty-two sevens."** That assumes that the seven sevens precedes the sixty-two sevens and after that the Messiah will be cut off. Since the Messiah cannot be cut off until he first comes, and that is not until both the seven sevens and sixty-two sevens have already occurred.

The first event listed after the pause in the counting of the sevens is a specific singular event; it is that **the Messiah shall be cut off, but not for Himself.** Jesus was crucified shortly after His triumphal entry into Jerusalem, so there is a very small time span between when the Messiah comes and when the Messiah is cut off.

The second event listed after the pause in the counting of the sevens is a specific singular event; it is that **the people of the ruler who will come will destroy the city and the sanctuary.** The destruction of the Temple and the city of Jerusalem happened several years after the pause in the counting of the sevens. Jesus presented himself as the Messiah in 33 A.D. and the Temple and Jerusalem were destroyed in 70 A.D., a time gap of 37 years.

The third event listed after the pause in the counting of the sevens is a general event that will not cease until the end has arrived; it is that **war will continue until the end.** The world is still in a state of war; therefore, the end of the prophecy is still in the future.

The fourth event listed after the pause in the counting of the sevens is a plural general event that has multiple fulfillments. It is that **desolations have been decreed.** There were many desolations of the land until there ceased to be any resemblance of a Jewish political entity until modern times when Israel became a nation again in 1948. In the interlude there was a huge time gap of about 1,800 years.

After the pause in the counting of the sevens and the prophecies that follow after the pause of the counting of the sevens, the counting of the last seven begins when the covenant with many is confirmed, as it says in verse 27.

Daniel 9:27

27 He will confirm a covenant with many for one seven. In the middle of the seven, he will put an end to sacrifice and offering. And on a wing (*of the temple*) he will set up an abomination that causes desolation, until the end that is decreed is poured out on him.

Interlinear NIV Hebrew-English Old Testament, John R. Kohlenberger III, (Grand Rapids: Zondervan Publishing House 1987)

The prophecies that the city and the sanctuary will be destroyed, which occurred in 70 A.D., and that desolations have been decreed, which was fulfilled when the Romans made Judea desolate in 135 A.D., precede the prophecy that he will confirm a covenant with many for one seven. Daniel 9:27 mentions the covenant with many *participants* and then an end to sacrifice and offerings and the setting up of an abomination that involves the Temple. Since the Temple was destroyed in 70 A.D. it would not be possible to put an end to sacrifice and offering and set up an abomination until a new Temple was built. Since 1948 when Israel became a nation again, there is a possibility of at least a small Temple being built in Jerusalem sometime in the future.

The covenant with many *participants* is still in the future. The covenant with many *participants* will mark the beginning of the seventieth seven years of the seventy sevens prophecy.

Jesus stopped reading in the scroll of Isaiah when he came to a time gap in the fulfillment of the prophecy.

Time gaps in long biblical prophecies are not unusual. For example, the Gospel of Luke describes an event where Jesus was reading a passage in the Book of Isaiah and when he got to a time gap in the prophecy, He closed the scroll. The passage Jesus was reading was Isaiah 61:1-2a, and then He closed the scroll because there was a time gap in the fulfillment of the prophecy. Isaiah 61:2b says, **"And the day of vengeance of our God."** There is a time gap between the fulfillment of Isaiah verse 61:2a and verse 61:2b. In Isaiah 61:2b, "The day of vengeance" did not apply at the time Jesus was reading the Isaiah passage in the Synagogue so he closed the scroll. Keep in mind that verse numbers did not appear in the original Isaiah text. Verse numbers were added to the Bible during the Middle Ages.

Luke 4:16-21
16 So He came to Nazareth, where He had been brought up. And as his custom was, He went into the synagogue on the Sabbath day, and stood up to read. 17 And He was handed the book of the prophet Isaiah. And when He had opened the book, He found the place where it was written: 18 "The Spirit of the Lord is upon Me, because He has anointed Me to preach the gospel to the poor; He has sent Me to heal the brokenhearted, to proclaim liberty to the captives and recovery of sight to the blind, to set at liberty those who are oppressed; 19 To proclaim the acceptable year of the Lord." 20 Then He closed the book and gave it back to the attendant and sat down. And the eyes of all who were in the synagogue were fixed on him. 21 And He began to say to them, "Today this scripture is fulfilled in your hearing."

Each time a Prophecy in the order of prophecies is fulfilled, we should be more and more assured that the next prophecy in the order will be fulfilled. Since the events before the time gap actually happened for real (in real life), we should be advised that the events after the time gap will also actually happen for real.

In Daniel 9:27 the **"He"** in **He will confirm a covenant with many** is **the ruler who will come** mentioned previously in Daniel 9:26. **The people of the ruler who will come** will precede **the ruler who will come** and they **will destroy the city and the sanctuary** before "He" even comes as the ruler because "He" will not come until after the desolations mentioned in Daniel 9:26. The future ruler will rule the people who destroyed the city of Jerusalem and the Temple and they were the people of the Roman Empire. Therefore, the future ruler who will make a covenant with many will rule the people of the Roman Empire that accrues after the Nation of Israel is restored. At the present time that is a possibility because the European Union has begun to cover much of the same territory as the ancient Roman Empire.

On the subject of the ruler who will come and make a covenant with many, Daniel 9:27 continues, **"on a wing (*of the temple*) he will set up an abomination that causes desolation."** That ruler is best known as the Antichrist as per I John 2:22, but he is also known by other names in other books of the Bible.

The Antichrist will begin with the smallest kingdom among ten kingdoms and he will uproot three other kings and take over their kingdoms for a total of four kingdoms. One of the kingdoms he will uproot and take over will be the European Union that already covers much of the same territory as the ancient Roman Empire.

The purpose for clarifying that there is a built-in time gap in the seventy sevens prophecy after the counting of the seven sevens and the sixty-two sevens is because some interpreters try to interpret it without allowing for the time gap and that leads to a gross misunderstanding that does not make sense.

Chapter 19

Israel a nation again in modern times—Israel becoming a nation again in 1948 A.D. marks the end of the desolation of Judea that began after 135 A.D.

Photograph by Rudi Weissenstein

When Israel became a nation again in 1948 and became a member of the United Nations in 1949 that was the first major sign that the time of the seventieth seven years as prophesied in Daniel 9:27 is near.

Revelation 11:1-2 speaks of measuring a temple without an outer court and since the Temple had been destroyed in 70 A.D. and Judea ceased to exist by 135 A.D., many Christians believed that Israel would need to become a nation again in order for a Temple to be built there again.

One of the earliest Christians that there is a record of writing that Israel would become a nation again is the mathematician, physicist, and Christian writer, Isaac Newton (1643-1727). However, prior to World War I and World War II, it was hard to fathom how it would be possible for Israel to become a nation again because prior to World War I the Ottoman Empire had been in control of that area since 1517 A.D.

On May 14, 1948, on the day when the British mandate over Palestine expired, at 4 p.m. in the Tel Aviv Art Museum under a portrait of Theodor Herzl, David Ben-Gurion publicly proclaimed the establishment of the State of Israel as of midnight on May 15.

Then President Harry S. Truman announced the USA's recognition of the State of Israel at 6:11 p.m. on May 14, Washington time, which was slightly after midnight in Israel. Three days later the USSR recognized Israel. After Israel's elections, de jure (according to law) recognition of the state of Israel was signed by the USA on January 31, 1949. In May 1949, Israel became a full member of the United Nations.

Source: *A Safe Haven,* by Allis and Donald Radosh (Harper Perennial, 2010)

Jesus used the parable of the fig tree to teach that the restoration of Israel is a sign that the end time is near.

Matthew 24:32-34
32 **"Now learn this parable from the fig tree: When its branch has already become tender and puts forth leaves, you know that summer is near. 33 So you also, when you see all these things, know that it is near-at the doors!**
34 **"Assuredly, I say to you, this generation will by no means pass away till all these things take place."**

The fig tree symbolizes the nation of Israel. The fig tree was alive for it had leaves, but after it was cursed it quickly withered away implying that the leaves fell off and it became barren. Jesus used the fig tree as an object lesson of what will happen to the nation of Israel.

When we interpret the significance of the parable from the fig tree, we need to keep in mind the overall context and the specific context. The overall context is that prior to telling the parable from the fig tree, Jesus had withered a fig tree and spoken about the Great Tribulation. The specific context of the parable from the fig tree is that it is primarily about a fig tree, not primarily about people. Jesus said, **"Now learn this parable from the fig tree."** In verse 34, **"this generation"** is the generation that saw the fig tree **"put forth leaves,"** as described in verse 32. Jesus is speaking directly to the generation that saw the fig tree put forth leaves, not necessarily to his own generation. Just as the fig tree that was cursed became barren, Israel became barren after the Roman army destroyed Jerusalem in 70 A.D., captured Masada in 73 A.D., and made Judaea desolate in 135 A.D. The parable from the fig tree presupposes that the fig tree goes through a period of barrenness before it begins to show life again as it sprouts leaves. In that same way Israel was barren for many years, and then in 1948 it became a nation again. The **"this generation"** in the parable from the fig tree that saw the fig tree bring forth leaves is the generation that saw Israel become a nation again in 1948-49.

Chapter 20

The Covenant or Treaty with many *participants* that marks the beginning of the seventieth seven years as prophesied in Daniel 9:27

The United Nations building may be where the covenant or tready with many *particpants* is ratified.

Daniel 9:27

27 He will confirm a covenant with many for one seven. In the middle of the seven, he will put an end to sacrifice and offering. And on a wing (*of the temple*) he will set up an abomination that causes desolation, until the end that is decreed is poured out on him.

Interlinear NIV Hebrew-English Old Testament, John R. Kohlenberger III, (Grand Rapids: Zondervan Publishing House 1987)

Before the Antichrist appears, there will be a falling away

The "**He**" that will confirm a covenant with many *participants* is described as the Man of Sin and the Antichrist. He will appear after the falling away. After the falling away, his unchristian, antichristian, doctrines will be acceptable to the general public.

2 Thessalonians 2:3

3 Let no one deceive you by any means; for *that day will not come* unless the falling away comes first, and the man of sin is revealed, the son of perdition.

1 John 4:3

3 And every spirit that does not confess that Jesus Christ has come in the flesh is not of God. And this is the *spirit* of the Antichrist, which you have heard was coming, and is now already in the world.

We are presently in the time of the falling away

The spirit of the antichrist is at work in the world and as the time of his appearance approaches, the influence of the spirit of the antichrist becomes stronger. At the present there are powerful unchristian antichristian modern influences coming from various directions and even young grade school children are exposed to unchristian antichristian modern thinking and ways. The thinking these days is we need to have something of everything and that leads to lawlessness; that is why the man of sin is called **"the lawless one"** in 2 Thessalonians 2:8. Notice, a way the spirit of the antichrist propagates his agenda, if you do not buy into the unchristian, antichristian, ways that are going on presently, you are called, "a hater". I wrote earlier that when the antichrist is on the earth there will be censorship of Christianity; however, that is

already going on. Some people speak of being on the right side of history. The trends these days during the falling away are not the right side of history to be on when the Lord Jesus returns again as the **Ruler**. Truly Isaiah 5:20 applies to our present situation.
Isaiah 5:20
20a **Woe to those who call evil good, and good evil.**

Now that Israel is a nation again the prophecies after the time gap are pertinent for our time period

Now that Israel is a nation again the covenant with many becomes a possibility. With the covenant with many the counting of the sevens begins again for one seven. In Daniel 11:28 and twice in Daniel 11:30 it is called the **holly covenant**. Calling it the **holy covenant** indicates that the covenant will have a provision involving the Temple. Revelation 11:1-2 describes a future Temple that fits the present conditions of the Jerusalem Temple Mount. Since the Muslim Dome of the Rock covers a substantial area of the Temple Mount, it seems there may be only enough room remaining for a small Jewish Temple without an outer court. The treaty may begin with a gathering of certain groups (the Abraham Accord for example), and then proceed to be accepted on a wider basis. A treaty that would allow Israel to have a temple on the Temple Mount site would need international support in order to succeed against certain factions that would be opposed to it. At the present time, the most likely place where such a treaty with many participants would be ratified is the United Nations.
Revelation 11:1-2
1 **Then I was given a reed like a measuring rod. And the angel stood, saying, "Rise and measure the temple of God, the altar, and those who worship there. 2 "But leave out the court which is outside the temple, and do not measure it, for it has been given to the Gentiles.**

Since the Temple may not have an outer court that leads to the conclusion that the Temple may be built in a small area and that the area where the court would be will be controlled by the Gentiles, much like the Muslims are in control of the Temple Mount at the present time.

When the antichrist appears, he will do signs and wonders and deceive many and who he is will not be apparent to those who do not know and understand the scriptures of the Bible.

The antichrist will be a participant in the covenant in some way, but who he is will not be readily apparent at that time, especially to those who do not know and understand the scriptures of the Bible. Those that have not received the Lord and have fallen away will be deceived by his lies to their own destruction.

2 Thessalonians 2:9-10
9 The coming of the *lawless one* is according to the working of Satan, with all power, signs, and lying wonders, 10 and with all unrighteous deception among those who perish, because they did not receive the love of the truth, that they might be saved.

The seventieth seven years of Dan.9:27 will be the time of the Great Tribulation spoken of by Jesus.

In Matthew 24:21 Jesus refers to this same period of time where He uses the term **great tribulation.** He places it in the future beyond His own time indicated by the future tense **will be** as in **there will be great tribulation**. It is a specific period of time that is unlike any period of time since the beginning of the world and unlike any period of time after it. It is a period of time of worldwide dimensions for if it were not shortened, no flesh would be saved. A Great Tribulation of that dimension has not happened yet. It is still in the future, but not very far in the future beyond our present time.

Mathew 24:21-22
21 "For then there will be great tribulation, such as has not been since the beginning of the world until this time, no, nor ever shall be. 22 And unless those days were shortened, no flesh would be saved; but for the elect's sake those days will be shortened."

The Lord Jesus will appear in the air and those in Christ (Christians) will receive glorified bodies and go to meet the Lord Jesus in the air.

The Lord Jesus will return again that where He is, we as those in Christ (Christians) may also be with Him.

1 Thessalonians 4:16-17
16 For the Lord Himself will descend from heaven with a shout, with the voice of an archangel, and with the trumpet of God. And the dead in Christ will rise first. 17 Then we who are alive *and* remain shall be caught up together with them in the clouds to meet the Lord in the air. And thus we shall always be with the Lord.

When the Lord Jesus appears in the air, He will shout a loud command and the trumpet of God will sound. The dead in Christ (Christians that have died) will receive resurrected glorified bodies like Jesus after He was crucified and rose from the grave. In His resurrected glorified body, He spoke to His disciples before He ascended to heaven where He is interceding for us. Christians who are alive at that time will also receive glorified bodies like Jesus after He rose from the dead. Then we shall ascend together to meet the Lord Jesus in the air.

Glorification

When the Lord Jesus appears in the air, and shouts a loud command, and the trumpet of God sounds, Christians will receive glorified bodies like Jesus after He rose from the dead as fast as the blink of an eye.

1 Corinthians 15:50-54
50 Now this I say, brethren, that flesh and blood cannot inherit the kingdom of God; nor does corruption inherit incorruption. 51 Behold, I tell you a mystery: We shall not all sleep, but we shall all be changed—52 in a moment, in the twinkling of an eye, at the last trumpet. For the trumpet will sound, and the dead will be raised incorruptible, and we shall

be changed. 53 For this corruptible must put on incorruption, and this mortal *must* put on immortality. 54 So when this corruptible has put on incorruption, and this mortal has put on immortality, then shall be brought to pass the saying that is written: *"Death is swallowed up in victory."*

The meeting in the air could occur at the present time or at any time in the near future.

We do not know when the meeting in the air with the Lord Jesus will occur. However, in the New Testament book of the Revelation, a great crowd from every tribe and nation is spoken of rejoicing and worshiping in heaven before the marriage supper of the Lamb. Furthermore, the marriage supper of the Lamb of God, the Lord Jesus, to the Church is spoken of as occurring before He returns to earth with the army of God and puts an end to the Great Tribulation.

In the Revelation, the marriage of the Lamb to the Church is spoken of before the description of the Second Advent of the Lord Jesus upon the earth at the end of the Great Tribulation.

Revelation 19:7-8

7 "Let us be glad and rejoice and give Him glory, for the marriage of the Lamb has come, and His wife has made herself ready." 8 And to her it was granted to be arrayed in fine linen, clean and bright, for the fine linen is the righteous acts of the saints.

Revelation 19:7 speaks of the marriage of the Lamb to his wife, the church. **His wife ἡτοίμασεν 'prepared' herself.** The Greek word ἡτοίμασεν is a 3rd person singular indicative aorist verb. The 3rd person singular refers to the church as a whole that is prepared. The indicative aorist indicates action completed in the past. The waiting is over, the Church is prepared, arrayed in fine linen, clean, and bright. The Revelation speaks of the wife being prepared before the Second Advent of The Lord Jesus upon the earth.

At the time of His second advent, the Lord Jesus will return, as the Ruler, in great power and glory.

The Lord Jesus will return to earth again in great power and glory with the armies of heaven. At that time, He will decide who has been on the right side of history.

Revelation 19:11-14
11. **Now I saw heaven opened, and behold, a white horse. And He who sat on him** *was* **called Faithful and True, and in righteousness He judges and makes war. 12 His eyes** *were* **like a flame of fire, and on His head** *were* **many crowns. He had a name written that no one knew except Himself. 13 He** *was* **clothed with a garment dipped in blood, and His name is called The Word of God. 14 And the armies of heaven, clothed in fine linen, white and clean, followed Him on white horses.**

In Revelation 19:10 the name of Jesus appears two times before the description of the Second Advent of Jesus. Verse 10b says, **"Worship God! For the testimony of Jesus is the spirit of prophecy."**

Christians will be with the Lord Jesus at the time of his Second Advent upon the earth when He steps upon the Mount of Olives.

Revelation 17:14 **"These will make war with the Lamb, and the Lamb will overcome them, for He is Lord of lords and King of kings; and those** *who are* **with Him** *are* **called, chosen, and faithful."**

In the context of the Lamb overcoming the beast, at that time Christians are with the Lord Jesus. Those who are chosen and faithful refers to Christians.

In Revelation 19:14 the armies in heaven following Jesus are clothed in fine linen, clean and white.

Christians qualify as members of the Lord's army since they washed their robes and made them white in the blood of the Lamb as described in Revelation 7:14; and since as the wife of the Lamb, they are arrayed in fine linen, clean and bright as described in Revelation 19:8.

When the Lord Jesus returns the surviving wicked will be judged.

Revelation 19:15
15a **Now out of his mouth goes a sharp sword, that with it He should strike the nations. And He Himself will rule them with a rod of iron.**

Revelation 19:20-21
20 **Then the beast was captured, and with him the false prophet who worked signs in his presence, by which he deceived those who received the mark of the beast and those who worshiped his image. These two were cast alive into the lake of fire burning with brimstone. 21 And the rest were killed with the sword which proceeded from the mouth of Him who sat on the horse. And all the birds were filled with their flesh.**

The Lord will return again and step on the Mount of Olives. From there the plain of Megiddo is only a moderate distance north. The Gentiles will be around about the area of Jerusalem. Revelation 19:15 speaks of the Lord striking the Gentiles.

In Revelation 19:20 the beast and the false prophet are cast alive into the Lake of Fire. The beast includes the seven kings of which the Antichrist is one king and the false prophet is the Antichrist viewed as an individual. The rest were killed by the sword from the mouth of Jesus, which may be symbolic of a verbal command. In Revelation 20:1-3 an angel casts Satan into the bottomless pit.

Beginning in Revelation 20:4, thrones are set up, the nations are judged, and the one thousand-year blessed Millennium begins.

Chapter 21
Misinterpretations that pervert the prophecies of Daniel

Matthew 24:14-16
14 "And this gospel of the kingdom will be preached in all the world as a witness to all the nations, and then the end will come. 15 Therefore when you see the *'abomination of desolation,'* spoken of by Daniel the prophet, standing in the holy place" (whoever reads, let him understand), **16 "Then let those who are in Judea flee to the mountains."**

The misinterpretation that Antiochus IV Epiphanes committed the abomination spoken of in Daniel 9:27

Secularists or modernists that call themselves Bible scholars know from history that Antiochus IV Epiphanes committed an abomination in the Jewish Temple in 168 B.C. when he polluted it with a pig, which is an unclean animal according to Jewish law. Then since they do not believe in biblical future prophecy or the inspiration of scripture, they claim that passage in Daniel was written after Antiochus IV Epiphanes.

Aside from a compendium of evidence based on the language such as the Aramaic section Daniel 2:4 through Daniel 7:8 is written in "Imperial Aramaic"[21-1] (an official language during Daniels time), and there are as many as "thirteen Akkadian words used in Daniel"[21-2] (an ancient language), plus the setting accurately places the writing of Daniel during the Babylonian captivity well before Antiochus IV Epiphanes, the ultimate answer is that the abomination spoken of in Daniel 9:27 is not even about Antiochus IV Epiphanes. It is about the future Antichrist. Antiochus IV Epiphanes was only a type of the future Antichrist. In Daniel 9:26-27 the abomination takes place after the destruction of the City of Jerusalem and the Temple.

Jesus is the Messiah and He has a perfect understanding of scripture. Jesus lived after Antiochus IV Epiphanes and Jesus placed the abomination spoken of by Daniel the prophet at a future time beyond the time when He was speaking about it, as recorded in Matthew 24:14-16.

21-1&2 History, Harmony & Daniel; E. W. Faulstich (Chronology Books; Spencer, IA) 11

The misinterpretation of combining the 70 AD destruction of the Temple prophesied in Daniel 9:26 and the abomination in Daniel 9:27 into one event

In Daniel 9:26 after the destruction of the City and the Temple there are desolations and a continuation of wars before the covenant with many for seven years in Daniel 9:27. Then in the middle of the seven years or three and one-half years later there is the putting a stop to sacrifice and offerings. After that, there is the abomination of desolation on a wing of the Temple. Furthermore, the Romans did not make a holy covenant with Judea.

The misinterpretation of claiming that in 135 AD, Emperor Hadrian committed the abomination spoken of in Daniel 9:27

Any act that the Emperor Hadrian may have committed does not qualify as the abomination spoken of in Daniel 9:27 because it was not preceded by a seven-year covenant and the Temple was already destroyed so he could not have put an end to sacrifice nor place an abomination on a wing of the Temple.

Ultra-figurative and anagogical interpretations that trivialize the prophecies in Daniel and Revelation

The visions in Daniel and Revelation are figurative in the sense that they contain symbols, but they are literal in the sense that they are about real events and the dialogue in the visions pertains to real events. Referring back to Daniel 9:26-27 the Messiah truly came for real, He was crucified for real, and the City and Temple were destroyed for real. Likewise, the future seven-year covenant with many and the abomination on a wing of the Temple will happen for real. The opening of the seven seals passages in Revelation, beginning with chapter six are still in the future; they are not historic about the past nor pertain to the ancient Romans. Revelation 17:12a says, **"The ten horns which you saw are ten kings who have received no kingdom as yet."** The ten kings spoken of in this passage are still in the future beyond John when he wrote Revelation, and they are still in the future beyond the present time.

Chapter 22
How to become a Christian

To become a Christian—one must repent, believe, and receive.

One becomes born again by repenting of one's own sins and exercising faith in the Lord Jesus Christ as one's own Lord and savior.

Ephesians 2:8-9
8 For by grace you have been saved through faith, and that not of yourselves; *it is* **the gift of God, 9 not of works, lest anyone should boast.**

1 John 1:9
9 If we confess our sins, He is faithful and just to forgive us *our* **sins and to cleanse us from all unrighteousness.**

Romans 10:9-10
9 That if you confess with your mouth the Lord Jesus and believe in your heart that God has raised Him from the dead, you will be saved. 10 For with the heart one believes unto righteousness, and with the mouth confession is made unto salvation.

Commentary

A popular conception of faith is that faith is a belief in something without proof. That is not Christian faith! Christian faith is something, or someone you put your trust in and live by! Living by faith is a commitment!

We are not saved by works we have done; we are saved by what Christ has done for us. According to the saying, "Not saved by good works, saved unto good works."

A prayer to become a Christian.

Walk the path of Faith

Acknowledge it is true
"I believe"

   I acknowledge that I am a sinner. I believe Jesus is the Lord. I believe Jesus is the Messiah, (the Christ). I believe that Jesus (who is the Christ) died on the cross and paid the penalty for sinners. I believe that Jesus rose again from the grave and lives forever more.

Receive it for yourself
"For me"

   My God and Heavenly Father, I repent of all my sins. Forgive me of my sins because Jesus paid the penalty for my sins when He died on the cross for me.
   Lord Jesus, be my Lord and my savior, and forgive me of my sins and cleanse me from all unrighteousness. Make me a new creation in Christ by the power of the Holy Spirit. Jesus, be my mediator before God now and on judgment day, and make me priest over my own soul.

Claim it as fulfilled and live accordingly
"Thank you, Lord"

   Jesus, thank you for dying on the cross for me and help me to live for you now and forever.
   In Jesus name I pray, amen!

Appendix

In the seventy sevens prophecy that speaks of a decree to rebuild Jerusalem that marks the beginning of the counting of the seventy sevens, a critical passage for determining that decree is in Daniel 9:25. The main sources are the Masoretic Hebrew text (900 A.D.) the Septuagint LXX Greek translation text and Theodotion's Greek version of Daniel as is in the Codex Vaticanus version of the Septuagint (300 A.D.). So far, only the early chapters of Daniel have been found among the dead sea scrolls.

The Greek version of Daniel written by Hebrew and Greek linguist Theodotion in 150 A.D. was preferred by some early Christians and Jews over the Septuagint LXX Greek translation (284-247 B.C.). Theodotion's Greek version of Daniel replaced the earlier LXX Daniel in the Septuagint as in Codex Vaticanus. Charles Lee Brenton's English translation is based on Codex Vaticanus and where parts were missing on Codex Alexandrinus.

Various translations of Daniel 9:25 in the Hebrew Masoretic text and the Greek Septuagint text

The Masoretic text (Hebrew)

2742	7339	1129	8145 (Strong Hebrew numbers)
וְחָר֑וּץ	רְח֣וֹב	וְנִבְנְתָה֙	תָּשׁוּב֮ ← read Hebrew
and ditch	(with) plaza	it shall be built	again

the street shall be built again, and the wall

The Interlinear Bible Hebrew-Greek-Eng., with Strong's concordance numbers above each word, Jay P. Green Sr., (Hendrickson Publishers, 1986) p. 691

The Masoretic text (Hebrew)

וְחָר֑וּץ	רְח֣וֹב	וְנִבְנְתָה֙	תָּשׁוּב֮ ← read Hebrew
and-trench	street	and-she-will-be-built	she-will-return

it will be rebuilt with streets and a trench

The interlinear NIV Hebrew English Old Testament, John R. Kohlenberger III, (Grand Rapids: Zondervan Publishing Houser, 1987) Vol. IV, p. 471

The Septuagint text (Greek translation)

Καὶ οἰκοδομηθήσεται πλατεία, καὶ τεῖχος
and   the street shall be built,   and the wall

The Septuagint Version of the Old Testament and Apocrypha with an English translation, by Charles Lee Brenton (Zondervan Pub. House, 1978) p. 1065 (Brenton's Septuagint is based on Codex Vaticanus)

The Septuagint Greek translation as in Codex Vaticanus (300-325 A.D.), of Daniel in particular, is based on Theodotion's Greek version (150 A.D.), who translated the Hebrew text he was using in his day into Greek as τεῖχος, **wall.** That is how the KJV and the NKJV translates Daniel 9:25 as **the street shall be built again, and the wall.**

Some modern versions have strictly followed the Masoretic Hebrew text (900 A.D.) and translated וְחָרוּץ as **trench** (NIV) or **moat** (ESV).

Although, Strong's Hebrew word number 2742 חָרוּץ 'hārûs' "a military defense," gives **wall** as one of the translation choices.

Conclusion

In Daniel 9:25, the concept of **it shall be built again** supports the Septuagint reading of τεῖχος, a **wall.** Jerusalem was known for having a wall before Nebuchadnezzar's army tore it down. In order to restore Jerusalem, the **wall** would need to be rebuilt again. Jerusalem was not known for having a **trench** or **moat** around it.

In most cases the Masoretic Hebrew text is preferred over the Septuagint Greek text of the Old Testament; however, in this specific case the translation **wall** has substantial historical support, but the translation **trench** or **moat** has none.

Various translations of Daniel 9:26 in the Masoretic Hebrew text and the Greek Septuagint text

Masoretic Hebrew text (Hebrew)

369

לוֹ   וְאֵין   ← read Hebrew

(Holem waw) Lamed   (Final nun) (Tsere yod) Alef (Vocal shewa) Waw
Ô l   n ê ' ĕ w   ← read English transliteration

Discussion of the translation of Daniel 9:26 in the Masoretic Hebrew text as **but not *for* Himself** as it is in the KJV and NKJV.

The Masoretic text (Hebrew)
          369   (Strong Hebrew number)

לוֹ   וְאֵין   ← read Hebrew

to-him   and is not
but not *for* himself
The Interlinear Bible, Jay P. Green Sr., (Hendrickson Publishing, 2013)

A direct literal translation of Daniel 9:26 is **"and *is* not to him"** or **"but not *for* himself."**

In the same book of Daniel as Daniel 9:26, the scholars Brown, Driver, and Briggs translate וְאֵין in Daniel 8:5 as: **"and (it) *was not.*"**
369

וְאֵין **"and (it) *was not*"** **touching the earth.**
Hebrew and English Lexicon of the Old Testament, Francis Brown, S. R. Driver and Charles A. Briggs (Clarendon Press: Oxford University Press) p.34

And in Strong's word 2050.2, וֹ may be translated **"him"** or **"himself."**
The Strongest Strong's James Strong revised by John R. Kohlenlenberger and James A. Swansen, (Grand Rapids: Zonderdervan Publishing House 2001) p. 1382

An example in the Bible is in I Samuel 8:11 where the simple לוֹ may be translated **'for himself.'**
I Samuel 8:11 **He shall take your sons and shall appoint *them***
לוֹ **'for himself'** **among his chariots.**

Conclusion
In Daniel 9:24 in the beginning of the preface, **"for your people"** (which continues on to speak of the work of the Messiah) supports the translation in Daniel 9:26, **"but not *for* himself."**

Discussion of the translation of Daniel 9:26 in the Masoretic Hebrew text as: **and will have nothing** as it is in the NIV and others.

The Masoretic text (Hebrew)

לוֹ   וְאֵין   ← read Hebrew

to-him   and-there-will-be-nothing

and will have nothing

The Interlinear NIV John R. Kohlenberger III (Zondervan Publishing House 1987)

    The translation of Dan. 9:6 as: "**and will have nothing**" is based on translating it as an idiom as Stephen R, Miller explains in NIV, *The New American Commentary, Vol. 18, Daniel* (Nashville, TN: **B & H** Publishing Group, 1994) p. 267 "The phrase 'ên lê is in Hebrew an idiom for "not have" (cf. Gen. 11:30; Isa. 27:4.)"

The translation of the examples given are as follows:

Isaiah 27:4a

חֵמָה אֵין לִי   חֵמָה אֵין לִי

me to not anger   me to not is fury

I am not angry.   **Fury is not in Me.**

John R. Kohlenberger III   Jay P. Green Sr

Genesis 11:30

אֵין לָהּ וָלָד

child her to not

Now Sarai was barren; she had no children.

John R. Kohlenberger III

אֵין לָהּ וָלָד

child her to no was

And Sarai was barren; she had no child.

Jay P. Green Sr.

    Notice that in the translation of Daniel 9:26 **"to him"** is omitted; however, in Isa. 27:4 **"to me"** is included as **"I am"** or **"in me"** and in Genesis 11:30 **"to her"** is included as **"she."**

Based on the examples, in order to be consistent with this variation of translation, Daniel 9:26 should be translated as "**and will have nothing to him.**"

Conclusion

A literal translation of Dan. 9:26 is "**and *is* not to him**" or "**but not *for* himself.**"

The translation of Dan. 9:26 as "**and will have nothing**" is not a direct translation of the Masoretic Hebrew text; it is a translation of the Hebrew as an idiom that several modern translators have chosen that does not fit the context. To say, "**will have nothing**" is contrary to the theological background as in Isaiah 53:8, **He was cut off for the sins of my people** and Isaiah chapter 53 as a whole.

Then in Daniel 9:24, the preface of the prophecy says, **"For your people"** and then continues on to speak of the accomplishments of the Messiah as it says, **"To finish transgression," "To put an end to sin," "To atone for wickedness," "to bring in everlasting righteousness,"** and that speaks of the work of the Messiah for the people, but not for himself because He is without sin and; therefore, He does not need to atone for Himself.

The Septuagint (Greek translation) of Daniel 9:26

καὶ κρίμα οὐκ ἔστιν ἐν αὐτῷ

and there is no judgement in him

The Septuagint Version of the Old Testament and Apocrypha with an English translation, by Charles Lee Brenton (Zondervan Pub. House, 1978) p. 1065 (Brenton's Septuagint is based on Codex Vaticanus)

καὶ   κρίμα   οὐκ ἔστιν ἐν   αὐτῷ
and   judgement   not it is in   in him

κρίμα means: a judgment; a judicial sentence; a condemnation. So, it could be translated as **and it is no condemnation in him.**

The eminent Greek language scholar Walter Bauer writing in German and translated by William F. Arndt and F, Wilbur Gingrich says concerning the Greek preposition ἐν under ἐν 4 d, "To denote a state of being (so freq. w. γίνομαι [I become], εἰμί [I am]."

A Greek English Lexicon of the New Testament and Other Early Christian Literature (The University of Chicago Press; Limited Edition, Zondervan Pub. House) p. 258

The preposition ἐν 'in' preceding the reflexive αὐτῷ 'in him' fits in this category of, "Denoting a state of being." In Dan. 9:26 αὐτῷ 'in him' is in the dative form, i.e. indirect object; therefore, 'him' is the object receiving the action of no (judgment or condemnation).

In Luke 23:39-41, the two criminals hanging on the cross speak of Jesus and κρίματι (dative singular form, i.e. indirect object form of κρίμα) is translated as **condemnation**.

Luke 23:39-41

39 Then one of the criminals who were hanged blasphemed Him, saying, "If You are the Christ, save Yourself and us." 40 But the other answering, rebuked him, saying, "Do you not even fear God, seeing you are under the same condemnation?

κρίματι

41 And we indeed justly, for we receive the due reward of our deeds but this Man has done nothing wrong.

Then Luke 23:13-15 speaks of Pilate and Herod not putting a judicial sentence or condemnation on Jesus as Pilate says, **"I have found no fault in this Man."**

Luke 23:13-15

13 Then Pilate, when he had called together the chief priests, the rulers, and the people, 14 said to them, "You have brought this Man to me, as one who misleads the people. And indeed, having examined *Him* in your presence, I have found no fault in this Man concerning those things of which you accuse Him; 15 no, neither did Herod, for I sent you back to him; and indeed nothing deserving of death has been done by Him."

Conclusion

So we see that in the Septuagint having Theodotion's Greek translation of Daniel 9:26 as: καὶ κρίμα οὐκ ἔστιν ἐν αὐτῷ (translated as) **and it is not (judgment** or **condemnation) in him** is fulfilled concerning Jesus in the New Testament.

In Theodotion's Greek translation in this phrase of Daniel 9:26 as it is in the Septuagint Codex Vaticanus Text (300 A.D.) is quite close to the Masoretic text with the exception that there is the inclusion of the Greek word 'κρίμα' (judgment or condemnation) that does not have the Hebrew word equivalent in the Masoretic Hebrew Text (900 A.D.).Theodotion was a Gnostic that converted to Judaism; he was not a Christian. Theodotion would not have had a reason to add a word to the Hebrew text he was translating. Theodotion's translation was popular with Christians and Jews of his day.

Brenton's translation was originally published by Samuel Bagster & Sons, London, 1851. It was republished by Zondervan with the Greek and English side by side. Hendrickson Publishing has also republished it. For the purpose of this study the Greek text is more useful than the English translation.

A New English Translation Of The Septuagint by Albert Pietersma and Benjamin G. Write (Oxford University Press N.Y., 2007). In the book of Daniel, it features side by side columns of an English translation of the Old Greek and Theodotion. In Daniel 9:26, the English translation of Theodotion is closer to the Masoretic text than the English translation of the Old Greek.

Index of Old Testament quotations New King James Version, Thomas Nelson

Front cover

Artaxerxes I giving letters to Nehemiah is a collage created by Douglas Ophus. The background is a photo of a floor at a mall, which is similar to the floor at Persepolis. Letter-size persons were drawn similar to reliefs at Persepolis, then scanned, cropped, and inserted into the background, which was in Microsoft Word. Nehemiah is based on reliefs of Hebrews. The collage was completed over a period of over two years and saved as a PDF.

The triumphal entry is a collage based on a photo of the Temple Mount taken from the south by Douglas Ophus with photos of himself inserted.

The Messiah, Jesus on the cross is a collage of photos taken by Douglas Ophus, which includes a photo of himself.

The Garden Tomb is based on a photo by Jason Ophus, which was altered with the large stone that was nearby pictured as inserted into the grove of the Tomb.

Photos of the Western Wall and the U. N. building are by Douglas Ophus. Two of the photos are apparently in public domain.

Back cover

The red moon over Golgotha is a collage created by Douglas Ophus based on a photo of the hill called Golgotha taken by Jason Ophus, which was altered and photos taken by Douglas Ophus inserted. The stars are those of Aries the Ram that appear in April.

For a description of the seventieth seven spoken of in Daniel 9:27 and the Revelation that is when the Great Tribulation will occur, read the book pictured below in grayscale, by the same author.